To Ann,

May audacious love
be with you,

Síochána,

Mary Jo.

Discovering Audacious Love

Finding Deep Happiness in Everyday life

Mary Jo Mc Veigh

BALBOA
PRESS

A DIVISION OF HAY HOUSE

Balboa Press books may be ordered through booksellers or by contacting:

Balboa Press
A Division of Hay House
1663 Liberty Drive
Bloomington, IN 47403
www.balboapress.com
1-(877) 407-4847

ISBN: 978-1-4525-0910-5 (sc)
ISBN: 978-1-4525-0912-9 (hc)
ISBN: 978-1-4525-0911-2 (e)

Library of Congress Control Number: 2013902844

Printed in the United States of America

Balboa Press rev. date: 05/08/2013

To the children of Belfast.
(As my mother said, Granny Gibson would have loved that.)

Pro tanto quid retribuamus.

Acknowledgments

Without the help and support of many people, this book would never have been written. There are many wonderful people in my life who believed in me when I did not believe in myself, held me when I could not hold myself, and loved me when I felt so unlovable.

I wish to acknowledge the following:

That ever present love that was, is, and always will be: my life source.

Clare and Jim Mc Veigh, for bringing my life into this world.

Clare Marie, Mara, Theresa, Margaret, James, and Roisin, for my belonging in this life.

Granny Gibson, Aunty Kitty, Aunty Molly, and Briege Bell, who blessed my life.

Matthew Rickard, who saved my life.

Cadhla and Conor, my reason for living.

Toby, our dog, who keeps on loving all of us.

Laura Luchi, who kept believing in my professional life.

Yvonne Barnes, who held my hand in that tunnel and who has been with me as I navigated my way through my new life.

Eric Hudson, who was reading as I awoke and who has dragged me into I don't know how many op shops since.

Alison Churchill, whose open door and open arms were ever there and whose hand I rested mine in when the fog lifted.

Cathy Howells, whose gentle "Don't make me come over there" would lift my spirits and whose "Drop and give me six" made me laugh.

Louise and Ray Barlow, who took me into their hearts long ago and then took me into their home, Toby and all!

Louise Goold, who rearranged my furniture as I rearranged my life.

The many wonderful friends who carried me through: Clare Craven, Connie Mac Dermott, Jo Whiting, Cathy Rawlings, Karen Smythe, Liz Morrison, Henrietta Foulds, Bronwyn Tuffey, Michael Lucey, Peter Gormley, Mary Anne and Alex Frigo, Terry Anderson, and Mark Hyland.

Cathy Want, Pam Swinfield, and Leonie Booth, whose generous professional hand kept a roof over our head until it was our time to move.

George, who showed me my scars were not something to be ashamed of but were the signature of my survival.

In the thirty wonderful years of my professional life, I have had many guides, teachers, and people who believed in me. You all allowed me to grow and become who I am today. I bring each of you into my work every day: Sally Simpkin, Shane Waterton,

Maureen Ledlin, Sue Mafi, Lesley Laing, Eric Hudson, and the Cara team (Laura Luchi, Naomi Illife, Julia Butler, and Sarah Dillane).

Thanks go to the many colleagues who sent me cards, flowers, and words of comfort. You brought my love of the profession back to life.

Particularly when writing the book, I would like to thank my dear friend, Alan, for many things, but especially for giving me the title for this book.

When I deleted the entire first edition, several people were instrumental and supportive in trying to retrieve it. Though it could not be retrieved, I was still shown great kindness by Miranda, Zoran, George, Matthew, Brendon, and Ben. On those days when I was writing and either needed to cry down the phone or just hear another human voice, Miranda was always there.

I appreciate Zoe, Sharman, Jennifer Butler, Liz Morrison, Lynn Moyce and Miranda Casella, who painstakingly gave form to some of my formless words so that others could read them.

To the team at Balboa Press, who, despite lost manuscripts, the tyranny of time difference for phone calls, and my lack of aptitude for the editing process, saw me through it all with grace and diligence. Especially Brandon Drake and Richelle Causing whose incredible support and hard work helped me through all the ups and downs.

I give you all my deepest gratitude and my *audacious love* always.

Contents

Introduction

Sacred Heart of Love, I place myself in you.
Sacred Heart of Love, place yourself in me.

From as far back into my childhood as I can remember, I was certain that I was born for a purpose other than being just a little girl from Belfast. I had no words to explain this internal knowing to myself, let alone anyone else, so while it was ever present, I never moved my lips to speak of its presence. So it patiently waited for its moment of release.

At the age of ten, that moment came. My sister told a story from a youth camp she had volunteered at, and again without uttered word, I knew what my life's work would entail. I was born to be in service of others.

The formal launch of my life in service started when I graduated from Queen's University Belfast with a master's degree in social work in 1986. My work took me from the city of my birth to London, Auckland, and Sydney, where I practised as a social worker in child protection and childhood trauma. After many years of work, I decided to write a book about it.

However, as the book took form beneath my keyboard-tapping fingers, I noticed what the book was not. It was not a clinical manual of "how to." It was not written from a place of certainty to tell people how to practise as a social worker or which technique to use. It has turned out not even to be a book for social workers.

To be truthful, I did not fully know what the content of this book was going to end up being. All I knew was that I was compelled to write it. I could not escape the persuasive voice that spoke to me of the words to be written. This voice of compulsion was not one of force or obligation but one of purposeful urging that let me know it would not stop until I wrote.

My own curiosity rapidly took over from this internal advisor to write. I was eager to find out what I would see as my emerging identity revealed itself to me from within the words I wrote. I was surprised to find that the beginning of my social-work identity started in early childhood. I originally sat down to write the first chapter about my days at university and was intrigued to find stories from my childhood flooding my thoughts. There were clear links to some of my professional principles being made to characters of childhood and they found their way onto the computer screen. I found a richness of knowledge that lay within my upbringing, a richness that deserves more recognition in my exploration of my personal growth and not just my professional development.

To my initial horror, I realized that this voice from my heart was coaching me to write not a clinical book but more of an autobiographical journey. I told some of my close friends of my trepidation at this discovery. They were fully supportive of the non-professional slant of the book. My further dismay that the initial editors of the book agreed with them seemed to strengthen their belief in the book's progress from clinical to personal. Therefore, I stopped running from it and agreed with this internal taskmaster to write the book you have in your hands today.

Discovering Audacious Love was started at a point in my life when I was coming through some difficult times. A time when I was learning to embrace myself as someone who, while committed to being part of healing the lives of others, was facing her own need for healing.

Embracing the "wounded healer" in me meant that I saw with renewed clarity the beauty in my own experience that could allow me to use my suffering in service of others. It allowed me to see that the pain and doubt that lay beneath the surface of my outward competence and assuredness was a great source of wisdom, and I could harness it. But more importantly, it shows me that if I could harness it, then everyone could. Not in a way that glorifies suffering or minimizes it but in a way that gives it its rightful place in our human journey, a place of dignity in the face of suffering.

So I wrote with a lessened embarrassment at my own autobiographical content. I wrote with a love that my words could be used to lessen the pain or confusion of anyone who might read them.

I wrote with a growing hope that people who turned the pages would feel that my suffering is the same arising suffering as theirs and they would know they were not alone. If I could ease but one person's loneliness, then this compulsion to write would make sense.

I wrote with a mounting passion about my discovery that joy exists despite pain, and it is accessible to everyone. If I could open up a new dialogue that allowed joy and pain to co-exist with equal honour, then the heart voice that directed me to write was wise indeed.

Within the following pages, you will hear my laughter and my laments. You will see my confusion and my clarity. In order for you to do so, I will show you snapshots of my childhood, relationships with colleagues, challenges in my adulthood, and experiences—painful and joyful, clinical and spiritual. I will lift back the veil of the personal to discuss the professional, and I will deconstruct the professional to find the personal. These are all honoured for what they are: my story. It is a story of deep and passionate love. A story of the discovery of audacious love in my life.

The title for this book came from something a dear friend of mine, Alan Jenkins, said. In the flow of a conversation, Alan asked of my two sons, "When did you realize your mother had this audacious love for you?" They enthusiastically answered (incredulously, might I add, as if being asked if they wanted a triple scoop of ice cream), "Always."

As I emerged from the surprise of the ease of Alan's question and the spontaneity my sons' answer, I saw how well they knew me. And then my thoughts flourished . . . Of course, "audacious love." Of course. The love I have not only for my sons and for people in my personal life but my relationship with my profession and with life itself. I saw that I dare to love with great courage and a dash of cheekiness, but I also have a relationship with a source of love: audacious love itself.

So, the big L word, the four-letter word that is so understood by many and misunderstood by many others! What is it about L-O-V-E, whose presence took my heart soaring to distant realms at some times in my life and whose departure left me crumpled on the floor, choking in gulps of chest-crushing pain? How is it that this one emotion can motivate or cripple? How can it open our eyes or blind us?

Love, love, love, love, love. So many great works of art are based on this single emotion: literary works, movies, fine arts, sculptures, buildings, landscapes, and the list goes on. And yet . . . how do we know what *kind* of love we are experiencing from minute to minute, what *kind* of love is driving us to make certain choices in our lives, what *kind* of love can pull us from the brink of despair and propel us towards a fulfilling and gratifying future? And why is it important to know the difference?

The word *love* seems to live on opposites ends of the earth when it comes to its use. It is rarely said when it should be or flung around in all directions from person to person without meaning. We are comfortable to say we love our favourite colour, yet we can't utter the word to the people we are sharing our lives with. We keep the word *love* for those who are close to us, yet people who are lonely or starved of affection or cast out by society never hear it uttered in their direction. We fill ourselves with the fire of love for our country and kill others in war in the name of it, yet we see it as weakness to say it to our children.

The most common thinking about love is of love as a feeling. Even in this definition, there are many far-reaching views. The feeling of love can mean to have a tenderness or friendship towards someone; it can mean having a liking or preference for an object or activity, or it can mean having a passionate or erotic attraction to someone. These are all very different feelings and are as dependent on who or what is receiving the love as it does on the engendering of this feeling. So love as a feeling has a physical and emotional component in our body and is delivered to another person in different forms depending on the relationship we have with that person: mother, sibling, friend, lover, or colleague.

I have come to see in my life that love is also more than a feeling state that is communicated through a relationship. Many of you will recognise that there have been times in your life that you either have loved someone but don't like what he or she does or you have experienced the feeling of love at a low ebb but you still relate well to someone. This brings the definition of love into the realm of love as an action—not just a feeling.

I am reminded of a day when my eldest son was about eight or nine years old. I was explaining to him why I would not give him permission to watch the adult-rated movies that many of his peers in school were watching. I told him that part of my role as a mother was to send him to school to nurture and develop his intellect and to feed, wash, and provide sleep routines to nurture and develop his body. I spoke of the family rituals and spiritual practices to nurture and develop his spirit. And I finally talked about protecting him from what I deemed as harmful situations (e.g., violent movies) to nurture, protect, and develop his heart.

As he listened to me, he burst out crying, holding tightly to my waist as my words continued. When I stopped talking, he looked up at me and, through gulping tears, said, "I know you are showing your love in many ways, Mama, and they are the right ways, but it is just *sooooo* hard sometimes." He buried his face in me to cry a lot more. He saw and could already articulate at this very young age love as an action and recognise how difficult this action can be at times.

Love as an action calls me to not only feel the energy of love flowing through my body as an emotion but also to consider how to act on behalf of another, how to do the work of love for the betterment of another. This love I have known and held tightly all my life through the teachings of the faith of my childhood, through the strong altruistic actions of my mother as she raised her family, and later through my practice as a social worker and trauma therapist for children and adults who had been abused.

It was much later in my life, when I was well into my forties, that I rediscovered another form of love: love as a presence. I became aware of love as a presence that is as real and tangible as the feel of warm water flowing over my body in a shower, the touch of the fabric of my clothing on my skin, and the pressure of seat bones on the chair I now sit on. I feel it inside me and all around me. Actually, it is more than a feeling: I am in its company. It exists as I exist. I feel it deep within me, within trees and mountains and rivers, residing within all living things. This is its *physical* manifestation. It simultaneously exists all around us. This is its *energy* manifestation. It is the heart of all things and within the heart of all things: a sacred heart.

This is a love that feeds my soul, has provided me with great healing during some very dark hours, and has allowed me to hold the hands of those I work with as they travel down their own paths of healing. A love that always challenges me to reach for new heights and never give up. This is a love that has asked me to take a risk to sometimes reap its rewards and sometimes feel pain, but it has always been of benefit to me.

It is a love that I not only feel or practise but am in a relationship with. It sustains me and enables all other forms of love to be possible in my life. This is the audacious presence of love.

As I wrote this book and formally acknowledged the power of my relationship with this presence of love, I was called to be brave. Living within and beside this presence of love asks me to be fearless every day because, after all, I am human with weaknesses and flaws. Discovering this love has allowed me to have the courage to risk falling and pick myself up with greater determination and confidence to try again . . . and again . . . and again. It is, after all, an audacious love. It took me over forty years to realise what my children already knew in that one word: "Always." It has always been present in my life and is to be found in many places, especially the unexpected and unsought.

The motto in the dedication of this book, "Pro tanto quid retribuamus," is the motto for the city of my birth: my beloved Belfast. The translated version I chose is this: "In return for so much, what shall we give back?" I have been given so many great opportunities, so many wondrous experiences, and so much love that I wanted to give back. This book is one of the ways I would like to give back.

For so much I have been given, I would like to give back in sharing the story of my journey of discovering audacious love in my life.

Chapter 1

Glory Be to a Belfast Childhood

Glory Be to Childhood
(A Tribute to Gerard Manley Hopkins)

Glory be to childhood.

For arms that held me when I cried,
the gifts of smiles from others,
for favourite food that warmed my soul,
and happy moments in midst of troubles.

For smell of rain on tarmac,
The rose that bloomed that day,
Finding lost socks and a clean T-shirt,
And for friends with whom to play.

Glory be.

It was amongst the Belfast people that I learnt about the horrors of violence and the need for peace and repair. I learnt about the oppression of colonization and the dignity of a human rights struggle. I learnt about the crushing of the human spirit and the joy of finding hope. My childhood in Belfast gave me bountiful wisdom about the human condition and how to navigate life's sorrowful and joyous journey, as well as a store of love to forage in. And it all started in North Belfast, a city at war in 1962, the year I was born.

The booming echoes of bombs and the images of violence were a daily reality. Even though my family lived in a quieter quarter of the city and did not awaken daily to the rumble of army tanks rolling down narrow streets, the permeating nature of violence was still thick in the Belfast air. I do not believe it possible to live in a city at war and not be touched in some way. Belfast saw some of the worst violence in its history, leading to the deaths of 1,500 people between 1969 and 2001. I lived in Belfast in this historical time from 1962 to 1987.

I remember feeling childhood light-heartedness instantly disappearing into my knotted stomach at the sound of a gun or a bomb. I remember the creeping dread up the back of my neck as adults huddled and whispered while discussing who had been killed. And . . . the spreading sourness in my mouth and bodily revulsion if I glimpsed on the six o'clock news the human carnage after a bombing.

Alongside this horror were the laughter of us kids in the street, the beautiful sight of the Cave Hill, which my home nestled beneath, and the smell of the salty air of Belfast Lough. I loved and feared my city with equal passion. I knew from an early age I was part of it, and it was part of me. Belfast—"Beal Feirste" in Irish—means "river mouth of the ford." As a city, she avalanches away from the foot of the Cave Hill, Divis, and Black Mountains, spreading out around the banks of the Lagan being halted by the salty water at the mouth of this river, the lough. This is my land. I could feel the pulse of the land Belfast was built upon under my feet. The vibration of her heartbeat was never quite drowned out for me by the relentless violence or industrialization. I loved her despite the malevolence that human behaviour stained her streets with.

Belfast's urban body was adorned by shipyards, factories, shopping areas, and residential areas of gardened mansions and rows of red brick houses facing each other in narrow, paved streets. She was festooned with parks and in places adorned with the grandeur of buildings, such as the city hall, Stormont, and the castle. I was raised in number 25, a small house nestled in the middle of a row of houses in an area of North Belfast called Greencastle. It is the home my mother and father moved into when they married, and they have remained in it for over fifty years.

It had three bedrooms, a kitchen, a living room, and a bathroom squeezed onto a rectangle of land with a small back garden and an even smaller front garden. The rooms were small and not overly crammed with furniture. However the energy of seven children wriggling and flapping like nested goslings made for a full house. When the washing machine was not on, piles of dirty laundry lay in heaps by the machine or stacks of washed clothes waited lop sidedly for the attention of a very heavy iron and old, battered, wooden ironing board. The transmitted noise from the black-and-white television at times gave way to the voice of BBC radio presenters—sounding very serious and knowing—competing with the chatter of several conversations or noises of us feisty children at play or in argument. All was enfolded in the aroma of vegetable soup, boiling tea towels, or burning coal from the open fire.

I loved the view from the front windows of our house: the Cave Hill rising up over our little street, her presence like the strong hug of a protective mother. And I loved the view from the back windows: the Belfast Lough stretching out to kiss the shores of the Hollywood Hills on the other side. At night when I looked across the lough, I could see the twinkling lights that civilization had dotted on the hilled landscape and imagined it to be a far-away, exotic land. As I sat staring out of the window, I allowed my gypsy heart to wander across the world and take me into jungles, up mountains, and through deserts. I dreamed to one day roam beyond the hills of my hometown. I did not know how this could become possible for a little girl from Belfast, but I enjoyed my dreams.

My family was formed by James Mc Veigh and Clare Gibson. They were a handsome couple. My father had glossy, black hair, keen, brown eyes, and a muscled body from his physical work in the family bar. While my mother carried weight in my later childhood years after having seven children, I thought she was the most beautiful woman I had ever seen. My early memories of her include a beehive hairdo, A-line skirts, and beautiful brown eyes framed with lines of black mascara and long, black eyelashes.

Clare and James Mc Veigh brought six daughters and one son into the world.

I loved my sisters and brother, and I while I cherished belonging to something special, a strange dissonance lay within me. The older ones seemed so knowledgeable, whereas the younger ones seemed so carefree and I didn't seem to fit on either end. They were all beautiful and talented to my adoring eyes. I did not see myself in this same admiring light; I just didn't seem to fit. I felt awkward inside and unattractive outside. I remember gathering at Granny Mc Veigh's house for Christmas and hiding behind a heavy, red-velvet curtain in the sitting room because I was so overwhelmed by the size and energy of the family gathering. I remember being teased that I was adopted because I looked so different from the rest of them and being engulfed by the pain of these words.

I cherished being part of them, and longed to be like them, yet I was so unalike. When I was about three years old, we were taken to a photographer for a family portrait. I clearly remember the terror when he brought the browning camera perched on a tripod in front of us. I burst into tears; I was chided for crying by my parents and teased by my siblings for many years for this sullen response to the camera. What this three-year-old me could not articulate was the fear I had that this dark machine would take my spirit. I knew it internally but could not express it externally. I kept this early sign of my "strangeness" secret.

Many years later, when I was in my late twenties, I stood in Kenya and was shocked by the sudden pull back to that moment in childhood when I was told of the discomfort some of the tribal people have about having their photograph taken; they believed it took their soul. In this abrupt transportation away from Africa to

Ireland of my past, that spiritual being that sensed my fear at three had found company on African soil. My body was consumed with a mixture of sadness about this long wait and elation that I was perhaps not so strange after all—well, at least not strange to the Masai Mara of Kenya.

Some years after that frightening childhood encounter with the camera another experience reinforced my self-deprecating weirdness. The family went on one of our many Sunday walks up the Cave Hill with my father. At one point on the walk, I ran ahead, and upon finding a path opening into the bushes followed it. I came to a cliff face and saw a man in a long, tan trench coat standing alone, his head repeatedly falling forward onto his chest. As it did so, it made a strange clicking noise. Screaming with fear, I ran back down the path and fell on the ground.

My father came running up behind me with a speed I had never seen him produce before and held me. When I told him of this ghostly figure, he asked what I thought to be a strange question. He asked if he touched me. As a child innocent of the abuses perpetrated on children, I did not understand why my father would ask such an irrelevant question. Of course, he did not touch me; he was a ghost. The amusement of my siblings told me quickly that seeing or speaking of such things was not normal, and because I enjoyed their company, I forced experiences like this go away. How did I determine it was a ghost? I just knew it was a ghost, just like I knew as I looked at a tree that it was a tree. Strangely, neither the path nor the cliff face existed when my father went to investigate. It was not until I was in my late forties that my father and I spoke of this incident again, both acknowledging the phantom and not the human condition of the man.

Silence was often my comfort when the dissimilarity between myself and others haunted me. The walls of our home were not insulated for noise, and so a place to be with my own thoughts was a luxury. I found my solitude hugged up against the wall under the back stairs. From this sheltered nook, I could stay quiet and even dry when it rained. I found solace and comfort in feeling my cold tipped nose bring to me my favourite cocktail of smells of clothes washing in marshmallow suds, salt air and snow resting on the Cave Hill. I could hear the muffled sounds of family life and be away from it but part of it at the same time. I could hear my mother's footfall as she moved around the kitchen and be safe in the nearness of her presence but be alone in the hidden contentment of my own company.

I was at times a shy and sullen child. I often favoured the safety of hiding behind my grandmother's velvet curtain or sought comfort in the unacceptable sucking of my thumb until too late an age. Sometimes, I would join in the family revelry and games with my siblings, and at other times, I continued to feel the lack of fit with them and withdraw into myself or want to be on my own. Life often confused and engulfed me with an intensity of energy that I found frightening. It was not anything in particular that seemed to trigger this confusion and fear, and it was never with me constantly. But it was with me more often than I liked.

At night, it would come when I lay in bed before I fell to sleep. I could sense the lives of the people of Belfast. I felt that someone was in pain, someone else was dying, and someone was being killed or doing the killing. I could feel people being born, laughing, and having fun. At the very moment of my sensing, a presence would enter my bedroom, and I feared it. I would cram any old thoughts into my head to keep it away from me.

During the day, this sense of confusion and fear would randomly come over me when playing or doing homework or household chores. To me other children seemed to know the rules of life and did not get these overwhelming thoughts that I got. It appeared that my siblings could not hear the suffering or joy of people around the world or sense the heartbeat of a tree as they walked past it. I silently doubted that they felt their chest bursting with joy when they saw the beauty of a butterfly or petals of a flower. I struggled already with being different. I told no one about these experiences as I practised more and more to be just like every other child I knew.

The contradiction of feeling part of and different was but one part of the wonderful kaleidoscope of experiences I grew up in.

I remember vying with my sisters to hold my father's hand as we walked up the Cave Hill or to visit Granny Mc Veigh. I remember the excited feelings of waiting to eat the weekly treat of chocolate after mass on Sunday mornings. There were the picnics, the family concerts in the front room, and the holidays to seaside destinations in Northern Ireland. Then there was the back garden often magically transformed into zoos, farms, and circus arenas by us children, when not used to dry out the loads and loads of washing produced by a family of nine. There was a lot of love and fun.

My father took incredible pride in running the family pub: The Railway Bar. As I write, I can see him bent over the steaming mop bucket which is carrying the smell of spilled Guinness to me. I watch his muscled arms with white sleeves rolled up moving back and forth over the barroom floor. He seemed to perform the mundane, menial tasks of running the bar with as much pride as he did when he served the customers and negotiated with deliverymen. I saw in this man's actions the nobility of serving others with so much pride that it seemed to me the most exalting work you could do.

I have not always had a relationship of ease with my father, and it surprised him when he read what I wrote about being influenced by watching him at work. And I was humbly grateful when he gave me his blessing to wrote my story.

I brought to my profession a love and pride in my work and a great belief in service to others. A belief that has sustained me, particularly on those days when clients seem harder to love, when the mundane tasks do not inspire me, and when the profession disappoints and I do not feeling like giving my all. It is on these days that "The Railway Bar school of wisdom" is strong and inspiring and I imbue the aspects of my work that I don't want to do with the love of service to others.

This childhood message I carried in me is of greater significance when I learnt as an adult that my father did not always like to work in the bar. He told me that he loved talking with the customers, but dreaded going in every day. His dread was that someone would plant a bomb in the bar. The bombing of public bars was all too common an occurrence in Belfast. While as a child I had harboured a silent, secret fear it would happen to my father's bar. I never knew until I was an adult that he had the same fear. Such is the limited knowledge of a child and the gulf that exists between parents and children. It is only when the child becomes the adult that the opportunity for sharing such secret dreads can happen, but isn't it wonderful that the fullness of time allows such connection?

And the dread came with devastating consequences. In 1974, when I was twelve years of age, someone placed a bomb in the side entrance of the bar and my father, upon seeing it, shouted for everyone to leave. We were all away at boarding school the night the bomb exploded. The morning after, I sat on the edge of my bed fully dressed with my hands in my lap, still with an eerie calmness waiting for my sisters to walk down the dormitory and give me the news that I knew already. I had dreamt about it in great detail the night before.

The years since the bombing have faded my memory of the detail of the dream but not the dream itself or the fact that I told no one of my dream. When they told me that morning, the explosion of emotions was audible in my cries. We travelled back home that day on the bus and arrived in Belfast early evening. As the bus moved past the devastation that once was the building that housed the bar, the knot in my stomach rose chokingly to my throat. I could hear a young man at the back of the bus say loudly, "It was about time that fenian[1] pub was blasted." He neither knew nor I suspect cared, that we sat amongst the other passengers on the bus. His sectarian hatred needed release, and my pain increased.

Upon arriving home, I saw my father sitting on the sofa watching himself on the evening news being interviewed in front of the bombed-out bar. My mother and Mrs. Murray busied themselves in the kitchen. There was a penetrating, silent pain cutting through the air in the house. I threw myself into my father's

---

[1]   Derogatory term in Northern Ireland for a person practising the Catholic faith.

arms, but he pushed me aside to watch the television. I was hurried into the kitchen, looking back to see his tear-stained face. My father was separated from us by a wall of suffering.

That day, when the family bar was destroyed in that sectarian bombing and people were killed and injured, I watched a part of my father die and never return. What I did not know in my child years but learnt in my adult years is that he carried a burden greater than not being able to rebuild the physical infrastructure of the bar. He felt responsible for the death of the young man who was his junior barman. To this day, feels he lives "on borrowed time."

From my childhood eyes that knew nothing of his sorrow, I saw only the distance that came between him and his family and the loss of my relationship with him. Our relationship repaired with the passing of time and the healing that distance from the immediacy of painful moments brings to relationships. His internal torment is something I cannot enter, but from my returned love for him, I have come to know and understand the deep scars that shattered dreams can leave on one's heart and spirit.

I saw that being trapped in the lived pain of yesterday would not change what had happened. I took from my father's anguish the courage to hold the pain of yesterday in a loving embrace and live within the next moments of life, acknowledging joy's eternal presence waiting for me to meet it again. It is in those next moments of life that possibility exists—that my connection to hope lies.

My experience of seeing my father's pain has emerged in my adult life in my ability to sit in compassion with others. I can witness their struggle but not be engulfed by it. I can be present in the healing relationship that honours the pain of past whilst holding the knowledge that growth is possible. This is the gauntlet that painful times throws down—to go through the pain and, when ready, allow life to continue and joy to flourish. This ability meant as a counsellor, friend, mother, and comforter to many people in my life, I was able to hold steadfast to the belief in the dignity of pain. It is a belief that allows me to be with people as they feel and come to know their own pain without the rush to bombard it with quick-fix solutions. But it does not abandon them to living under the oppression of past pain.

Towards the end of writing this book, I fractured my right wrist—awkward as a right-hander! The day after the plaster cast was applied to my arm, the build-up of pain was so severe that I was dizzy and nauseous. I had lived with the nagging pain of the fracture, but the quality of this pain was different so I made an appointment with a fracture clinic. When the clinician removed the plaster to reveal a trapped nerve in my hand, she congratulated me on getting myself into the clinic so quickly. Any further delay could have led to more severe, if not permanent, damage. My friend commented on the good fortune that I did not use painkillers, as I would have masked the pain and not sought further help. I shared with both of these women my belief in listening to what the pain was telling me to do rather than masking it. The nagging pain in the wrist was the pain of repair; the sickening pain was the pain of ongoing damage. This little moment in life was not lost on me. The words that I was putting to this book and the message I heard in the wrist pain merged in life's synchronicity.

My mother's influence on me has always been obvious to me. She is a powerhouse of strength and courage that as a child sometimes made me cower, but as an adult, I appreciate and deeply honour it.

I see myself when I was about three or four clinging onto my mother's pinny[2] and peeking out from within the safety of its fabric at an alien being I had never seen the likes of before; he was sitting on our back doorstep. His dirt-smeared skin had the glisten and thickness of the smeared paint on an artist's pallet. His weathered, sculpted facial features made it hard to know his age, but looking back, he could have been between forty and seventy. His clothes were stiff with the starch of months of body sweat and street grime, and his odour had a sickly pull to it. I studied him with wary curiosity. He seemed different, not of us, somehow

---

[2]   Childhood name for an apron.

"other." Occasionally, Belfast's homeless population was seen in the appearance of older men we called tramps, but they were often seen in the centre of the city, not in the homes of ordinary people. I somehow knew that every other door in our street would have been closed in this man's face. Yet here he was as if appearing from nowhere on our back doorstep. After eating he seemed to disappear to, returning to that nowhere from which he came.

As he sat on our doorstep, my gaze went upwards to my mother. I watched her actions of handing him the cloth to wash his face and giving him food. I cannot remember what she said, but I felt in her words and saw in her face that I was witnessing something of depth. As a child, I had no intellectual anchor to moor myself by, but I knew I was in the presence of something truly beautiful. I was in awe of this presence, what I now know to be my first experience of grace.

My mother took pride in her domestic skills, and I thought she had not brought him into the house because of the cleanliness of our home. But discussing this memory with her years later, she corrected my assumption by telling me that upon inviting him into the house he refused. He did not want to bring his dirt in with him.

I saw in this woman no fear, no disgust, and no sense of being "other" to him. It was my first exposure to the depth of human love and compassion. I saw the act of giving that so moved me that, over forty years later, I still hold the significance of the moment. My mother taught me in that moment an experiential definition of love—a universal, timeless, accepting love. A love that brought me into direct connection with all of humanity. A love that showed me that each life I touch, each opportunity to connect to another person, is a chance to show human compassion and love.

Social-work training taught me the art of using counselling skills and some very useful frameworks for professional service delivery, but my mother gave me the enduring gift of love for humanity. A love most needed when people are seemingly at their most broken, most unclean, their most unlovable.

I cannot lay claim to demonstrating this depth of love every day of my personal and professional life. I bring to my work and relationships with others the humanness of my own brokenness and imperfection, which at times invites me into the more judgmental side of my being. But I do know that I carry this love deep within me. It glows and shines at times with varying intensity, but it is never extinguished and is increasing with the passing years.

The gift of hope was given to me by mother and father in very different ways. It lies within my spirit as a gentle energy that enables me to see beauty despite the ugliness of violence and abuse. It lies in my knowing that the possible is always there.

My mother was accustomed to nurturing seven children and running a family home on a very restricted budget. Treats and extravagances were confined to shared chocolate bars after mass on Sunday, the occasional punnet of strawberries sliced so thinly and spread on a sponge base so that nine people enjoyed the summery flavour, or powdered desserts to take with us on summer holidays. What my mother did not do when it came to buying treats was to buy for herself. So when she came home from work one day with a twig enshrined in plastic, I was curious. My curiosity moved to intrigue and questioning why my mother, who is such a sensible person, would buy a dead twig and think it is a rose bush! I then watched (with the silent, patronizing sympathy of a child for a deluded parent) over the months as she worked the clay in our back garden to massage it into a form ready to receive the dead twig, and then she tended the twig to make it ready to become a rose bush.

I will never forget seeing the first nipples of green slowly appearing all over that "dead twig" and the first deep red rose that blossomed the following spring. Some forty years later, I can still feel the physical impact of seeing that beauty, that incredible beauty. I saw this beauty not just in the rose's petals and its perfume but in my mother's soiled hands and heavy dig. I could not believe that something so beautiful could grow from such inconsequential beginnings in our tiny garden. On that day, as surely as my mother put that cutting in the soil, she planted in her daughter an ability to find beauty in the human spirit alongside the deadness that sorrow and pain can bring. She gave me my formative lesson in hope, which has endured and sustained me in my life.

My relationship with hope is not a whimsical sentiment. It is a hope that works as hard as my mother did with the soil, that tends to life as she did with the digging and weeding and pruning. It is a hope that believes that growth is possible—not definite but possible—and most certainly worth the hard work. A hope that can be harnessed and used as a force for growth.

There can be no story about me without acknowledgement of my grandmother, Tessie Gibson. Granny Gibson was (and after her death still is) one of my main sources of strength and guidance, and I owe my love of learning to her. She passed on to her daughter, my mother, and then on to me a thirst for knowledge and a yearning to be the best that I could be. In my times of doubt, ignorance, or lack of strength, I turn to my grandmother. And in conversation, we always find a way through.

My relationship with Granny Gibson was pure love. I loved her with a childlike affection that is a precious currency to have in life. My mosaic memory of her recalls with a huge sense of joy the most delicious bread-and-butter she would offer us when visiting, her wrinkled and folded skin that was soft and reassuring to the touch, her Christmas tree that sparkled brighter than any other, and her quirky habits that amused and comforted me.

For me now as in childhood just to be in her presence, I felt love. She did not do anything that I can describe to you of great significance that formed my adult identity. I do not recall any great words wisdom that guided me on the pathway to my future.

I could recount stories my mother told me about her great strength and intelligence and how she helped so many in the community. While these stories of her life very much reflect who she was, they are not my stories of my relationship with her. My story of her is simply one of loving her and being loved by her, and from this love all else grew.

My godmother, Kitty Gibson, was another source of great love in my childhood. She was my living angel of grace. I thought her to be so beautiful and elegant. I saw myself as an awkward, scrawny, and not physically attractive child, so her graceful presence was a boon to my childhood. When I need to find my grace or acceptance of my own brokenness, I still turn to her in silent conversation many years after her death, and she still doesn't fail me.

I remember playing hide-and-seek at my cousin's house when, without warning, my happiness was swamped by my reoccurring, overwhelming feeling of being baffled by life. No matter how I fought this perplexity, it pushed me away from feeling connected to the game and into the house to find myself standing beside Aunty Kitty at the kitchen sink as she peeled potatoes. With flawless movement that never broke the rhythm of her peeling, she involved me in this domestic task. She put another potato peeler into my hand, passed me a potato, and continued the up and down scrape on the potato skin. Without either of us speaking, I joined her. I do not remember any more details from stepping up to the sink other than the fact I felt connected again. She seemed to know exactly what I needed without speaking, without drawing attention to my awkwardness, and without expecting some explanation or acknowledgement in return. She made me safe to be me.

With her, I was not so out of step with life and ill fitting in my skin. I was not so scrawny or ugly and possibly could even achieve elegance or gracefulness. Who knows? All I know is I simply drew comfort from being in her presence.

Mrs Bell, a woman from our parish in Belfast, gave me a similar gift. I was ten years old the summer she took her family on holiday in the same seaside town that we did were staying at. Unknown to me, her husband had recently died and she was a woman carrying the burden of this loss. What I clearly remember upon meeting her on the first day was that I needed to be by her side. There was a pull to be with this gentle woman whose quiet voice, small stature, and fine features seemed to accentuate her mildness. I eased into a silent pleasure in her company, wanting only to be near her. Looking back through time, I do not recall any conversations we had or wisdom imparted from adult to child. In fact, in my memory, we spoke very little, but being with her was wonderfully peaceful.

I simply enjoyed the energy of her company, an emotional jigsaw piece fitting perfectly into my heart.

We touch base very irregularly now that I live over the other side of the world from her, but I went to visit her when I returned to Ireland in 2011. She is aging and not in good health, and I am now an adult who has no child need to be met by her. Sitting with her, I felt the connection stronger than I had in childhood. It went beyond physical presence into the very spirit of who we both are. The child she knew grew into a woman who was able to tell her of the spiritual connection I have with her. Our conversations had been sparse throughout the years, and yet here I was talking of spiritual significance. And with the same acceptance I had received from her silently in childhood, I now received in her gentle smile and acknowledgment of what I was saying.

What a glorious gift to be given by life in the embodiment of Mrs Bell. The gift of human presence that has a power in itself beyond any actions, any words, and anything we try to achieve. Mrs Bell is my beacon of the power of presence. This power, I believe, lies within the spirit of who each of us is and should never be discounted. It is a gift we can all give.

Aunties are such great life teachers, and another one of mine was Aunt Molly. She did not have the grace and gentility of Aunt Kitty. She drew me in, sometimes with horrified glee—she was, after all, the first woman I ever saw drink beer. She would entertain me with stories of all the family scandals. I was, and still remain, deeply fond of her. I spent a lot of my formative years in her company, as she took care of us when our parents were at work.

From within this mildly outrageous relationship, she held up to me a mirror in whose reflection I saw my own integrity. She noticed this in me and storied it within some sections of the family for me to find years later as an adult. It all came about through balls of wool!

Aunt Molly was rarely seen without knitting needles in her hand, perhaps only put them down to make us her famous Aunt Molly stew. She was like my mother and father—not replete with money and so when she gave me money for something I needed, she did so knowing I had none to give her in return. I knew too that she had not much to share. As a known knitter myself, a neighbour gave me some wool she had to spare—Aladdinian treasures in my hands. I gave them to my aunt. All these years later, I cannot remember what I said to her, but I felt a sensation of something significant stirring deep inside me. It is still within me. I could see on her face what I can only describe as appreciation. Her response then, and in her often retelling the story to some of my other aunts and uncles, told me there was something honourable in what I had done.

The word *integrity* was only put to my actions years later when I was told by my mother that I was known within the family circle as a person of integrity because of the storytelling of Aunty Molly. As a child, I did not intend to reach the lofty heights of integrity, but I did want to *do the right thing*. It seemed important to me at the time; it just felt right. Her reactions not only further cemented my belief in doing the right thing but also made this a characteristic part of me.

When I get feedback from colleagues about my work, I often hear the word *integrity* put to my name and I pause. I always wanted to normalize without minimizing this part of who I am. Recalling this relationship with Aunt Molly allows me now to explain the simplicity and the beautiful ordinariness of learning integrity through balls of knitting wool.

If it was the women of my childhood and the one man, my father, who laid down the firm foundations for my future work in life, then listening to a conversation between my sister, Mara, and my mother brought the defining moment when I knew what I had been born to do.

I was no more than ten or eleven years old when my sister volunteered at a holiday camp for what was then termed "underprivileged children" from across the north of Ireland. On the day of her return, she was talking with my mother about her time at the camp. I sat nearby, my attention moving in and out of the conversation. She began to recount an incident at one of the mealtimes when a young boy pulled a knife out to attack one of the workers when he got into a rage during a mealtime. The boy was no older than me. I was perplexed at the level of anger Mara was describing in his swearing and lunging at the staff member with the knife. I thought that that level of violence was the domain of adults and we children just squabbled or hit out harmlessly. Though she continued to talk, I do not recall any further description of the incident because her words had penetrated deep into me and I could feel him. I knew he was in pain, and my initial surprise at this action turned spontaneously to compassionate care.

The strength of knowing he was struggling stayed silent within me until the moment I wrote those words, but it is as strong now as it was some forty years ago. I knew I was somehow connected to him and would be with children like him for a very large part of my life.

I never voiced it, as I feared replies of "Sit down and eat your porridge," "Button up because it is cold," or, worse still, "The bank is a good, steady job for a young girl to go into." In fairness to the adults in my life, I never gave them the chance to encourage or discourage me; my fear kept me from sharing my belief with anyone until much later in my life. To be born for purpose seemed too lofty an ideal for "just a little girl from Belfast," and so I censored myself. While I may have stayed silent about this belief in my purpose and I was unsure where I got the certainty of the message from, I just know it hung in the air of my life. It was invisible but no less present than the smoke that hung in the evening air from the coal-fired chimney tops of every Belfast home.

That day when I heard my sister speak, I knew this was what I had been waiting to know, the portal through which I would find a way to do what I was born to do. I was born to ease suffering and bring love to people, especially children. In my child's mind, I had no name for it and no way of knowing how to go about living my born purpose. I had never heard of the professions of social work or counselling, but I knew my time would come. And as sudden as my realization came, it went. I got up and went out to play as if this was a day like any other day for me. And then I forgot this experience until many years later when I was to write about the influences in my professional development.

While this was a pivotal moment in awakening my future identity, the ongoing nurturing of it occurred in the streets of Belfast, school, and family from the moment of my birth. A slow realization has dawned with the passing of the years. It is a realization that while learnt knowledge resides securely in my intellect, my lived knowledge from my Belfast Irish legacy lies deep in my spirit. It is the spirit of who I am.

It seems to me that too many of us either demonize our childhoods or romanticize them. We either shed them emotionally as clothes soiled from a day's wear or cling to a Peter Pan version of them. Through my dawning years, I have come to see the wisdom of my childhood not as fact or fiction but as a deep well from which to draw thirst-quenching water. This wisdom, born of both joy and sorrow, is a formative love, a solid platform from which the unfolding years of my life were built.

Chapter 2

Of Books and Boys

While I spent my early childhood years in the 1960s on the streets of Belfast by 1974, when I was twelve, I went to boarding school outside Belfast in the Mountains of Mourne. While I missed being at home with my mother and father, the loss was not as penetrating of my heart because I had four of my sisters and several of my cousins with me. Any loss I felt was ameliorated by the beauty I was surrounded by. Though I loved my city, the grey streets of Belfast were swapped for green fields and mountains, and I got to go home at the weekend to my parents and my beloved Belfast. Life was in perfect balance.

In my adult life, I listen to stories of abandonment by people who experienced boarding school as parental rejection. My mother poured her financial resources into educating her children. My story of going to boarding school was one of parental love and my returning gratitude. It deeply hurt my mother to see us leave every week, and it caused great financial stress. But she believed that she was giving her children the best educational opportunity she could—away from the overcrowding of our tiny house and the violence on the streets of Belfast.

My time at St Louis was a time not only of academic pursuits and religious instruction but also a time when I grew from a child to adolescent and into a young woman (not all in a seamless flow). It was a very tumultuous time for me. I had a great group of friends, and we shared the joys of the youth culture of 1970s: rock and disco music, wide-bottomed trousers, sporting and social pursuits, and of course boys!

Relationships with boys, however, were treacherous territory for me. I was a skinny teenager with long, lank hair, freckles, crooked teeth, and a deep awareness I was not physically attractive to my male peers. Physical attraction was unfortunately a sought after commodity for mainstream youth culture then as it is today. My cheeky personality, humour, and ability to talk to anyone masked the anguish of knowing that other girls had their strings of handsome boyfriends and romantic stories while I was perhaps destined to be the daughter who stayed at home and looked after her parents. There seemed to be a mixed message in Ireland of my childhood. Loyalty to family was important, but the spinster left at home was viewed with pity. I had enough layers of negativity about myself without adding that one to the pile.

At sixteen, when I did join the lucky set of "girl with boy," I picked a boy who was older, not from the same religion, and drove a motorbike—not exactly boyfriend material for a young Catholic girl! But for a time, I was head over heels in teenage love and shoved my lack of self-esteem into the back seat of life. After nearly a year, it ended abruptly when he unexplainably cut off all contact. With aching heart, I got back to living with my lack of self-confidence again. Despite this descent back into singledom again, I found solace in sport, friendships, a growing spiritual consciousness, and an overwhelming attraction to pacifism in the face of the violence of Northern Ireland.

Navigating relationships with girlfriends was easy for me, with only a few mistakes made along the way. Some of my friends turned to me in times of difficulty, and at that young age, I had a budding ability to ease them and a quirky sense of humour. Night routines were strict in the boarding school and because I had a friend in my room after lights were out, talking her through a problem she was facing, I got removed from the luxury of the senior bedrooms to sleep a few nights in a junior dormitory. Regardless of the consequences that night, I learnt some actions that break the rules are still worth it!

As I grew into adolescence, my desire to travel was awakened by my beautiful sister, Margaret. She spoke enthusiastically about a school trip she had made to Spain. The thing I remember most about this conversation, and that held me in a trance, was when she described seeing an orange tree. I was familiar with the fruit lying in a bowl, I had seen images of orange trees in books and on the television, but there was something much more magical about seeing the fruit on the tree. As she spoke, I drew a picture in my mind of a thick, gnarled branch adorned with green leaves and bowing under the weight of golden orbs of orange. My heart ached with the desire to see if for myself. I had to wait only two years before the little girl that I was, who sat with chin in palms looking out over Belfast Lough, longing to travel, got her first chance.

When I was sixteen, I went to France with my sisters, Theresa and Margaret. Theresa was nineteen, Margaret was eighteen, and we three wonderfully naive but intrepid young women headed off one summer to hitchhike around France. For those who have traversed the world in greater distances, this may not seem like much of a journey. But for us, it was an adventure and for me, it was my first taste of land that was not Irish. I loved every second of this holiday: the people we met, the unacquainted smells, the different tastes, and the small mishaps that we later laughed about. The unfamiliarly of this country excited me and drew me to more. But to enjoy this "more," I had to wait until early adulthood.

At that time in my life a greater awakening than travel was my spiritual awakening. I received a Catholic education throughout all my schooling but at grammar school I was taught a form of Catholicism I had not previously been exposed to. The God of my early Catholic childhood was, to put it frankly, a bit scary and very judgmental. Everything seemed to be about not doing the wrong thing, following the right rules, being a good girl, which were lofty spiritual heights I never seemed to gain at the age of five or eight or ten. I feared that my childlike misdemeanours of telling lies or stealing a lolly would incur the wrath of a male deity and I would be eternally punished.

At St Louis, one religion teacher in particular, Mr Ryan, offered a different God to me. I learnt of a Christ who worked to alleviate injustice and pain and who felt his place was amongst the disenfranchised, the poor, and the disregarded. I fell in love with this Christ and the work that he did. I was not only introduced to a political Christ and a Catholicism that had a social justice framework, I was also introduced to the life and wisdom of such figures as Martin Luther King and Mahatma Gandhi. My internal world was expanding and my soul were being fed. I loved this refreshing approach to my faith. As well as having more formal religious instruction, we would listen to the lyrics of popular music to find meaning and personal inspiration.

I remember listening to Simon and Garfunkel's "I Am a Rock" and using the lyrics as a springboard to discussing the value of human connections and the dangers of individualism. I remember hearing Paul McCartney's "Let It Be" and still, to this day, turn to lyrics when I feel in despair. We attended class retreats away from academic instruction to discuss theological and social issues. This formative training in reflective and contemplative practice is still very much a part of my life and my way of nurturing my heart, mind, and spirit.

One truly pivotal moment in my spiritual awakening stands out for me above all others. It was when I met Mother Teresa. I had gone with a group of young people from both sides of the religious divide in Northern Ireland to a peace community for a youth gathering. The international acclaim that my country attracted in the media never included these moments of great solidarity and a desire by many of us to see peace in our land. I firmly believed then, as I do now, that the actions of the peaceful many are as important as the actions of the violent few, even if not recognized or reported as newsworthy by junked-up media of this world.

Mother Teresa's exact words have faded in my memory with time, except for one thing that rocked me in my standing spot. She stood in front of this ragbag collection of young people and spoke of how humble she felt to be in our presence because, as she saw it, we had come together despite the supposed hatred that should exist between us. I had to listen to the repeated echoes in my head of her words to make sure I heard them correctly. Our presence was the source of her humility. I couldn't quite get my head around this. I saw this beautiful, compassionate, and caring woman who dedicated her life to helping others in extremely difficult situations be humble before someone like *me*, just a little girl from Belfast. She was talking to the me who carried the recent image of being told by a nun at school that I was nothing but a "dirty Belfast stone thrower who lowered the tone of the school" (despite the fact I never threw a stone at another human being in my life!)

As I stood beside her and shook her hand, almost towering over this tiny woman, I looked into eyes that overwhelmed me with their beauty. In this proximity to her, I was bathed in an energy that was strong in its presence but gentle in its nature. I stood in the manifestation of pure love.

Alongside my spiritual and religious upbringing as a Catholic, I also experienced a different form of spirituality, one that was born of a deep connection with the land. At the time, I had no name for this; however, in later years, I recognized it as the innate Celtic spiritual soul that I was born with.

I could hear the heartbeat of this glorious planet rising up from the earth's core through the soil to her surface. As a child and adolescent, I would often lie with my ear pressed against the earth, hearing and feeling the pulse of the earth's heartbeat. I would touch trees and feel a vibrant energy flow through the bark to my hand or hear messages in the screech of a crow. I knew without doubt that this was a living planet full of a divine energy source. I was in awe-filled love with it and was left at times breathless by its power.

This soulful Celtic connection to the land caused conflict within me. Whilst being connected to the divine presence in nature felt very normal, almost unnoticeably ordinary to me, I also felt ashamed as if there was a kind of wrongness attached to me. Catholicism certainly let me know to indulge in any form of worship outside the rituals of the church was forbidden. I wondered if my connection to the land was this forbidden worship. I was acutely aware of the word *pagan* being associated with all things evil, and this seemed akin to what I was doing. I confided in no one and lived for a very long time in silence with my own "wrongness." From within the Catholic faith, the poetry of the Jesuit priest Gerard Manley Hopkins gave me some comfort. But I was not spiritually mature yet or exposed to the works of the mystics, so I remained in my silent wrongness until much later in my life.

The social justice theology, the divine power of the land, and the call to a spiritual existence, though silent, stayed strong within me as I moved out of my teenage years to a life at university. However I began to find less and less connection to the practices of the Catholic Church. I struggled with a male-dominated religion that did not work to share the spiritual space with my gender and within whose institutional practices the abuse of woman and children were evident.

I continued to practise Catholicism intermittently, hoping I would find a renewed faith, wondering if I could be as devoted as members of my family or those I saw around me at Sunday mass. I really did not want any other cause to feel different. So long before I stopped attending the ritual services of the Catholic Church, I knew that my spiritual journey would not always be under the canons of this faith.

During my undergraduate years, I moved into student accommodation in South Belfast, within the university district, with three other girls from my high school. I was enrolled in Queen's University Belfast to do an arts degree majoring in sociology. The days were spent going to lectures or the student union building engrossed in conversation, more about the latest social event than major academic ideas. Participation in social events, playing sport, and hanging out with friends became the order of my life. I was enjoying this student life style so much that conscious spiritual awareness was not on the agenda. I no longer felt out of step or different from others. I was just another student at Queen's having fun and going to lectures when late nights and socializing permitted.

My self-consciousness about my physical appearance had not left me, but it was masked under a shaky self-confidence that having had a few relationships with young men brought. In 1981, I met a young law student called Padraig, and I fell in love for the first time in my life. His dark, chiselled features, obvious intelligence, and humorous personality captivated me. He was a beautiful young man who grew into a good man and lawyer who went on to help many people in his beloved city of Derry.

Months that folded into several years were spent in a relationship that I cherish deeply. I remember being with him one night in the winter of my second year. An evening fall had left a thick blanket of snow on the streets of Belfast. After leaving one of the bars in the students union, I joined a group on the steps of the union building in a snowball fight. It was just before the Christmas holidays and our relief at the end of exams and anticipation for having a break at Christmas left us all in high spirits. We were still young enough to revel in the delights of the snow.

The May Ball marked one of the most important university events on the social calendar. I can see myself walking home in the early hours of the morning dressed in a light-blue, strapless dress and Padraig in his formal attire. My feet were sore from wearing shoes far too high, my body slightly aching from long hours of dancing, but it was of minor consequence to the fun we had enjoyed. I turned to look into his handsome face and thought that this was as happy as I could get, and perhaps this was the man I would live my life out with.

Before that moment, my awareness of love as a feeling was for family, friends, the land, and the divine inspiration of Mother Teresa. But this was a new love; this was love for a partner. Life had expanded my view of love yet again and allowed me to experience it in connection with another, an experience I am deeply grateful for.

While my undergraduate years at university may be described as a time of learning more about hedonistic pursuits than the forming of any professional identity, they were not wasted. I was exposed to ideas from sociology, philosophy, anthropology, and psychology. These ideas grew within me and demanded that I think more for myself, that I form views and opinions. That I think, think, think!

In my third year of study at Queen's, I volunteered at a local refuge for women and children escaping from domestic violence. I worked with the children, and the social worker I was to formally become three years later awoke. I graduated with my undergraduate degree in 1983. I applied to do the master's degree in social work. However, the faculty staff who interviewed me felt I needed more practical experience than the short stint volunteering at the refuge. I applied for a job as a volunteer supervisor with Voluntary Service Belfast in June 1983 and spent until August 1984 in that post, working in the community in North Belfast. My role was to assess the request for practical help and organize a team of volunteers to complete the work.

This was a crucial year of maturation for me and the continuing hiatus of some of the happiest and most carefree years of my life. I was not only in full-time employment, but I was entering the lives of people to help them. I began to appreciate more and more the bounties of my family and the benefit of my education. I developed a wonderful relationship to gratitude that allowed me to see the beauty of the gentle, compassionate, loving person in me. I also had the pleasure of working with a great team of people. In particular, I formed friendships with Camilla, Andrew, and Aldo, with the former two remaining dear to my heart. We not only worked well together helping our community throughout the entire Belfast metropolitan area, but we would enjoy many social events together.

In 1984, I reapplied for a place on the master's degree in social work at my former university and was accepted, along with twenty-four other students. (Four—Marie, Cindy, Anne, and Sarah—became lifelong friends despite the tyranny of miles that stand between us now.) From October 1984 to June 1986, I lived my life in bliss as a social-work student. I lived with my sister, Margaret, back in the university district of the city. My sister was a skilled and compassionate paediatric nurse at the children's hospital, and so our flat was conveniently located for both of us. I shared my time being with her, my student friends, and Padraig. Our flat was a hub of social life for all of our friends. We had dinner in, evenings out, and mutual friends coming and going. These two years living with my sister multiplied the happy years of my young adulthood in Belfast to six. Six great years of fun and growing, loving and learning from all that life had to offer. We not only learnt together but we lived our lives together, and even though it was for a short time, much love and learning stays with me today when I bring to mind all the people who were in my life at this time.

On the academic side of life, the various theories that paraded themselves in front of me stimulated my mind. Some I connected with and found meaning when some of life's complexities made no sense. Others I fervently rejected when they seemed dehumanizing or silencing of people's unique experience.

In my social-work training, I was determined to dedicate my life to helping people and doing it well. I had found what I was born to do, and in doing so perhaps would not feel so out of step or "wrong" as I had felt in early childhood.

I did not excel in the academics of social work, often panting across the finish line in subjects like statistics. However, in my report on the completion of my master's degree, it was noted, "Mary Jo's practice skills were commended by all three practice teaches who assessed her skills were of a high quality. Her dissertation achieved an exceptionally high mark."

The fact that the practical application of my degree came with ease never surprised me. I simply loved what I did. I developed as a passionate, hardworking social worker who chose to work in child protection and child trauma. I found my work gave life an added meaning, and while not all days were fun filled, they were jam-packed with purpose. I felt blessed to have this fervour for my work; it sparkled in my day-to-day existence.

Despite finding my passion and purpose in a worthy vocation, my wonderful relationship with Padraig, and my great group of friends, I was feeling restless. My Celtic gypsy heart started beating a little louder, and I had the urge to go travelling. I wanted to see the world outside Northern Ireland and do some voluntary work overseas, perhaps for a year or longer.

So in November 1996, with no more than a small suitcase full of clothes, I stepped on to an aeroplane to London with my friend Sarah. I said a permanent goodbye to the young man I had been in love with for five years. I said a temporary goodbye to my family, my friends, and my beloved Belfast. My heart was screaming, "Ouch!" I didn't realize that following my dreams to travel would cause so much pain, but it did. Even though I was initially only going to London, which was a short distance from Belfast, it hurt with a pain I had never experienced before. I never doubted it was what I wanted to do. I just felt ambushed by the depth of pain that lodged itself stubbornly in my chest. And yet resting at the top of my heart, on the upper tip of the pain, was a sense of excitement and fun to be had. That's the thing about some feelings. You don't know you have them until the contrasting version of them appears. I've met my own courage when I've been most afraid, and here I was stepping onto that plane, feeling my greatest elation when I felt in most pain.

Chapter 3

The Leaving of Belfast

Upon arriving in London, Sarah and I first stayed with her friend, Geraldine, in the borough of Tooting Broadway in the south of the city. It was from this crowded but safe base that I started to explore all that this vast city had to offer me. London was exciting. It was a patchwork quilted with new sights and sounds and happenings. I approached every experience with a naive excitement—long live the joy and wonder of naivety!

What I loved most of all was that it was awash with cultures and ways of life so totally different from my upbringing. I can still faintly feel the gentle tug of a comb through the long, straight hair that fell down my back as a young Jamaican girl I was caring for brushed it. She was fascinated by its texture and wanted to experience brushing this hair, as it was so different from her own tightly curled black hair. Her request to brush the hair of the other members of staff who were white was not met with agreement, as they felt it not appropriate professional behaviour, so I obliged. As her hand moved in slow up and down strokes, she picked up the courage to ask me why God had not given me any colour in my skin. Then ensued the first of many spiritual conversations with children I have had spanning thirty years of my life and half the globe.

A recent holiday experience sparked my memory of this interaction. Each day I watched for two cranes along the stretch of beach where I was staying. I would see them every morning and evening standing side by side, fishing side by side, and flying off together in unison. The beauty of this couple being illuminated in the aqua light of the lagoon, one a black-feathered body and the other white. I wondered out loud to my children if these two birds noticed or cared about their different-coloured feathers. I thought of myself and the young Jamaican girl and felt again the beauty of human connection and how this beauty should not be ignored. If only humanity could connect like this all the time.

One of my most enjoyable and unforgettable jobs was as a residential social worker in a children's unit. It was home to five children who had been deemed by children's court and the child-protection system to be in need of care by the state due to the actions of their parents. The age range of the children was between ten and sixteen years old. Our small staff team worked a roster of day and night shifts and we often worked on our own.

My most memorable shift, and probably the one that catapulted my learning from the academic world of social work to the real world of social work, was my first night shift alone with these five children. The fun began after dinner when the sixteen-year-old told me she was leaving for the night to stay with her boyfriend and the other four children disappeared. With my heart beating faster than was imaginable with the thought of the harm that may be happening to the children whom the state had placed in my care, and my career finishing within its first year, I checked the documentation to seek guidance on what to do when the entire resident group went missing. I was to call the local police station after making all reasonable efforts to locate them.

As the police officer on duty answered my call, I poured my predicament out to him. I was bemused when his first question was whether this was my first time on night shift. I could not see the applicability of this question. These vulnerable children may be at risk, but I answered dutifully that it was. He then asked me to check behind a clump of bushes and get back to him. It was as the dial tone indicated that the phone had been hung up that the relevance of his question dawned on me. I peered over the hedge to find four giggling children and then felt relief mixed with annoyance at my initiation ceremony.

My five years of rigorous academic and professional training did not automatically kick in. Instead, I found myself standing with my hands on my hips and spoke in a manner reminiscent of the times my poor, exacerbated mother had to chastise her naughty brood. It was an exacerbation of relief born from a place of deep love, and here I was, a professionally trained person, feeling the same relief for the safety of these children. I noticed that I really cared about them and feared any harm that may come to them, but I felt conflicted by the place of my professional training in empathy and the spontaneity of tapping into feelings of genuine love and concern. So I started to enrol in training courses. I wanted to know more than I was taught at university. I wanted to be the best I could be and figure out how to be more professional, be more effective, and love in a more professional way.

After working at the children's residential unit, I held a job at the 226 Project for two and a half years. This project in South London worked with young people at risk of going into state care or youth custody due to their behaviour at school or their risk taking or offending in the community. If my work with the younger children ignited the spark of my love for my work, then my time at 226 certainly fanned it into a flame of passion. I entered a steep learning curve in my skills and knowledge under the management and guidance of Sally Simpkin and the companionship of my colleagues: Mary, Hugh, Liz, and Chris, as well as the professionals I worked with in the education, justice, police, and social services agencies.

I clearly remember my introductory meeting with a young person named Kay.[3] I was mildly terrified to meet a young woman who on paper read to be highly volatile at best and very dangerous at her worst. She had been expelled from various schools for violence and was very resistant to any professional intervention that had been offered. When I met her, I found her to be energetic,

---

3   In deep respect for all the people I have worked with, I will be using pseudonyms and changing minor details.

quick witted, fast tongued, and so vulnerable to being hurt it was written all over the hardened face she scowled at me with. I found myself liking her. I liked the fact that she was not going to be pushed around by a bunch of well-meaning adults, me included, who wanted to tell her what to do with her life. I liked the fact that she had opinions on what she wanted and she voiced them, albeit in rather colourful language! I liked her strong sense of justice on matters to do with young people. I simply liked her. Over the two years, I was fortunate enough to work with her, it was a privilege to be allowed to hear her childlike laughter, see the beauty of joy in her eyes, take part in her successes, and mostly, see the scowl replaced with a look of trust when she looked into my face.

My preliminary meeting with the first boy I had responsibility for was filled with equal trepidation. His short life of fifteen years was a series of abusive and traumatic events. He let none of this story be known by his words, but his repeat offending brought the judgement of society and professionals on his head and he faced juvenile detention. Over the years I worked with him, I had to appear at Wimbledon police station and juvenile court on more occasions than I care to remember. I always did so in compassionate silence and mindful of my duty to help him find another path in life. One late afternoon when I went to collect him from the police station to take him back to the children's home he was living at, he looked at me with a sadness that was weighted way beyond his fifteen years. He said, "How come it is always you, Mary Jo, you who is there for me? It's not my mother, not my father, not my social worker, but you. Thank you." It felt like a knife had been slashed across my heart as the pain of his abandonment coupled with gratitude moved from his heart to mine.

I recall another time when I was not so patient in my duty to him. I showed him my annoyance at his behaviour in an overly stern way, raising my voice not quite to a shout but certainly with less respect in it and more exacerbation than there should have been. After I walked away and had time to reflect, I returned and apologized to him. I explained that while I did not agree with his offending behaviour, it was not my role to judge him but to guide him. I expressed my regret for the lack of dignity and respect I had approached him with. His eyes welled with tears, and as a large involuntary droplet rolled down his cheek, he gasped that no one had ever apologized to him before or expressed the desire to be respectful.

I saw in that moment a young boy showing his vulnerability and appreciation for being held in the dignity of his humanity, and I saw myself as his equal, seeing no reason why I should not hold him in respect. I remember another boy telling me he turned around his violent behaviour because I believed in him when others did not. I was almost speechless but managed to squeeze out of my mouth, "But who am I not to believe in you or anyone?" It is this form of exquisite humility I meet time and time again in my work, those moments of deep connection that allow grace to enter into the world.

Though I know myself to be a loving person, life has also shown me the vengeful one who lives within. I know that part of me that does not want to forgive those who have hurt me. But greater than this desire is my commitment to seeking a path away from punishment. I am far from perfect so often fall short of my own compassionate intentions. When I do I call for help. I ask for the grace of compassion when working with these young offenders. I steadfastly seek a relationship with grace that allows me to navigate through the times I stray from my beliefs in forgiveness over revenge. The first step I learnt in doing so was to forgive myself when these feelings arose in me and to love the pained person who wants to hurt those who have hurt her. I meet my less-than-perfect self with love and self-acceptance and bless the space between each of these parts of me. It is from this blessed space that I can access forgiveness.

After working at the 226 Project for over two years, I decided to move within the local borough to take a job as a child-protection social worker. I was fortunate to be guided by Paddy Mc Nally, whose advice to breathe before making any major decisions on children's lives, while not seeming to be a clinically sophisticated choice, was one of the most useful pieces of advice I have been given in my career.

While my role with children was more assessment and investigative in nature, I found I had a natural ability to communicate with them and a flair for finding creative ways to connect. I attended several excellent training courses on working therapeutically with children and completed my family therapy training. A new form of love entered my life again. I fell in love with all things therapeutic and finally knew I wanted to spend the rest of my career working therapeutically with children.

While my budding career was blossoming, my social landscape was expanding exponentially. On my days off from work, I would visit art galleries, museums, parks, and the famous and historical buildings of London. And of course, I shopped. I ventured into pubs, clubs, and restaurants and delighted in my social confidence and ability to chat to anyone. I approached all of this with a natural sense of fun and wonderment, seeing all my social experiences as an adventure, eager to see who I would meet next. My more worldly colleagues cautioned me for what they saw as my naivety, sometimes playfully teasing me as I would show delight at chatting to someone only to be told that I was being—as they termed it—"hit on." I could never see that myself. I was just having fun, dancing, talking, and getting to know people and myself in the process.

On one such social adventure, about a year into being in London, I went to a party with a friend. I knew no one else at the party beside my friend and her boyfriend. However, that did not deter me from stepping into the middle of the dancing crowd and becoming lost in the sheer pleasure of moving my body to the rhythm of the music. I cared not that I was dancing on my own, for at that stage I had no idea where my friend was.

The party was in someone's home so the floor space for dancing was at a premium. As I like room to move my dancing body freely, I was ready to defend my tiny patch of floor with exaggerated swinging hips and moving arms. I was doing so well until a well-formed male bottom invaded my dancing space, and attached to it was the man I was to marry some two years later. I recall his friend telling me some years later that he assumed that we had known each other before the night we met, because as David turned to face me, we spoke with such ease and comfort.

The next two years with David were packed full. We went to every major theatrical production we could get to. I saw actors I had only once dreamed to see, from Daniel Day-Lewis playing Macbeth to Dustin Hoffman's Shylock. We sat in the front row for *Macbeth*, and as Daniel Day-Lewis stepped onto the stage, my body gasped in air. It felt like I held that single inhalation throughout the whole performance.

We went to see the major Russian and English ballet companies: the Kirov and Bolshoi and the Royal and the National. For my first ballet, I sat in the front row waiting eagerly for Giselle to start. When the troupe came floating on the stage to the tap of pointed toes and the gentle swish of tutu, I saw poetry written in the movement of human body, and slow, soft tears trickled down my glowing cheeks. They did not stop until the first intermission. I never thought that I would see such beauty of physical form on a stage. I still can't believe it. When I went to see art exhibitions, I would stand mesmerised in front of a Kandinsky or Monet and wish that my unbroken gaze would last forever. I was mesmerized by beauty in all of its forms.

During these moments of gazing upon such exquisite works of art, I felt more like the little girl from Belfast than the woman I was. During my childhood, I always believed that these experiences belonged only to the privileged few. The few who had the means to access this world of beauty and who seemed to have an air of entitlement, not children from the streets of a war-torn city. Yet here I was. While I feared that I might be uncovered as a fraud who did not belong, I also knew I deserved to be there just like anyone born into wealth or social status. But the most exciting thought, and the most comforting thought I had, was that if I could access beauty, then any little girl or boy from Belfast—and any other part of the world where pain existed—could access his or her version of beauty. This filled me with overflowing joy and a sense of hope that I kept in private storage in my thoughts, until now that is (☺).

David and I would also visit Kew Gardens regularly to delight in the green and colour of trees, flowers, and plants that the grey streets of London did not provide. We would also visit his family in Herefordshire and take my favourite trip to North England to see my sister, Theresa and her family. We would make the long car trip as often as we could to spend the weekend indulging in the joy of being with my nieces, the humour, and the great cooking of my sister. My younger sister, Roisin, subsequently moved to the same area so we would see her also. It was good to have family in England, as it brought a piece of Ireland, and of course the family, closer to me.

As well as discovering the landscape of England, I had three holidays in Europe over the five years I was in London. Two of these holidays were with David: one was skiing in the Italian Alps and the other was a spring break in Venice. I also took a week to myself in Rome. As before, these holidays, while vastly enjoyable, did not satisfy what seemed to be an insatiable hunger for travel. As I noticed this continuing desire to travel farther afield, I also became aware of my longing to live back in Ireland. I missed the quality of the light in her day, the lushness of her land, and the enfolding energy of my own people around me. An ache to return sat alongside a yearning to travel. Some twenty-six years later, these seemingly conflicting pairs still live in my heart, but I now trust that time will let me know when each has had its day. I look over my shoulder at my life of fifty years and know that all I did was as it should have been. To stay in Ireland was not to be part of my story, but to stop loving her and my people was also not there. I will continue to love my life and all the places I go, and I will cry when the ache of missing her returns.

The fun, the beauty, and the adventures were also at times tinged with sharp reminders of what it meant to be Irish living in England. For the most part during my time there, I was met with great warmth and love by people, but there were times when a clear cultural divide was obvious—with the Irish being in the inferior position to the English. This was particularly true for the Northern Irish, especially when the continuing violence would claim the life of a British soldier. I would have to listen to people on TV and radio, read in printed media, and overhear in the general public that all Irish were terrorists, and I would recoil in horror at the news of yet another police raid on the homes of Irish families. With people I knew in England, it felt safer, but at times, the gulf between us would open up but never be spoken out. I learnt to hide my Irishness, soften my voice in public, and pretend not to be offended at the telling of derogatory jokes against my people, for fear of being seen as militant or worse: a terrorist. That's called survival.

One of the boys I was working with spoke of his ambition to join the army and go to Belfast and kill all the Catholics he could find because his friend's brother had been killed by the IRA. When I told him I was born into the Catholic faith, he told me he didn't want to kill me because he liked me. With humour as my entry point, I told him most of my family still lived in Belfast so he agreed not to kill them. I then told him of my extended family. He agreed not to kill them. I then told him about my friends who were still there, and he agreed not to kill them. I was about to tell him about other Catholic people I knew when he asked me in rather colourful terms if I was related to every Catholic in Northern Ireland. I said yes to divert his future planned killing spree.

In this and other experiences in London, I saw the power of separation. The story this boy was recruited into was one in which the Irish were seen as inferior and the enemy. The reverse also happens in some families in Ireland. I do not think we are born thinking this way. I think the randomness of life places us in family, in county, and in culture, and socialization kicks in. Hatred and war can only exist when "other" is created. Without an enemy, there is no war. Create an enemy, war continues. My parents have nurtured in me an honouring of being Irish but not a hatred of others. As a result, I continue to be fiercely proud of my Celtic ancestry but never picked up a weapon of war to defend this and chose the way of peace.

In October 1990, David and I got married in my home parish of Greencastle in Belfast. It was important for me to begin my sacred contract with the man I chose to spend my life with in my spiritual birthplace. The parish of St Mary in Greencastle had seen me and my siblings through all the major rites of passage of our Catholic upbringing, and I wanted the significance of this imbued in my wedding ceremony. And it was. We were married by my dear friend and parish priest from London. My family was involved in every aspect of the ceremony and reception. I was amongst my people, on my land, and offering my life to another. It was not just a wedding day; it was one of the most significant spiritual rites of passage of my life. It was a rite of passage that was a public sign that we had chosen each other for life. Uncle Sean spoke of me at the reception as being "a dutiful daughter, a dutiful niece, who would make a dutiful wife."

Some years later, when I was telling people about what Uncle Sean had said, they expressed horror on my behalf. They felt sentiments like this trap women in relationships of sacrifice and continue to perpetrate a male-controlled view of marriage. My growing knowledge of the socialization of men and women into this patriarchal view of marriage and my abhorrence of this reality for women totally understands this take of what Uncle Sean said. However, in this context, this was not the meaning I took from his words, and as his words were meant for me, I see great love in them.

My take on his words, my meaning, is a pronouncement of my belonging to my parents in love. As they fulfilled their responsibility in raising me from childhood to adulthood, it is my glad duty to honour that and love them for it. In entering a sacred contract with someone for life, I wanted to do the same. I see it as an honour for two people to jointly undertake to love, support, and nurture each other. This is the sense of duty as a partner I took on the day I married David and left Ireland to begin my live with him on the other side of the world. The source of this honourable love is no different from the duty of love I saw myself give to the young people I worked with the five years in London. No different from the love I gave my sisters when I went to visit them in the north of England and no different from the love I gave to the friends I made in London.

The practice of the love as it comes through me is different in terms of how I relate to the various people in the different parts of my life. However, the source inside me that wants to love is the same, and if it is given the name by some as "duty," then I for one don't mind that at all.

Chapter 4

Our Mary Jo from Jakarta

When we left London, we had our six-month plan for travelling to Australia. We just didn't have our visas! Time had gotten away from us, and as the date for our wedding and departure approached, visas for Australia still had not been finalized. With a wedding fully organised, travel itinerary set, and tickets booked, we decided to stick to our original departure date and collect our visas in an Australian consulate somewhere in Asia. I am always intrigued by those moments in life when, despite what I think about my own nature, I act in contradiction to it. Heading off to live in Australia with no entry visa on my passport could definitely be defined as one of those moments.

Over the years that David got to know me, he learnt of my love of the natural world. I would tell him of the hours I was glued to the TV while watching every natural-history program that was put to air. I shared my admiration of David Attenborough, boasting of ownership of many of his books and videos of his programs. I laughed as I told David about my love of biology being so strong that at one point in my childhood I dreamed of being a marine biologist or being as famous as David Attenborough as I traversed jungles or climbed mountains. I realized there was not much need for a marine biologist in Ireland. But thankfully my other great love flourished, working with people. So with his understanding of this love of mine, David arranged for us to go to Kenya on safari before we headed to south-east Asia. He kept the destination secret from me until we got on the aeroplane. When it registered where we were going, my heart burst open and the yearning to travel that had been locked in there for all those years escaped. That little girl in me took her chin out of her hands and her gaze away from the Belfast Lough. She planted on my adult face an impossibly exaggerated grin. *I was going to Africa.*

When we got off the plane in Mombasa, the heat that bounced off the tarmac nearly pushed me back on to the aeroplane. Then the air enticed me forward with unfamiliar smells whose exotic bouquet left no doubt that I was far away from Belfast. My excitement was a little muted by the exhaustion of the hype of the days running up to the wedding and then the long flight. But it was present nonetheless.

We stayed in a comfortable hotel for a few days to recover before heading off on safari. The first part of the safari was spent in Amboseli National Park that stretched out from the base of snowed-capped Mount Kilimanjaro. The vast, parched, dusty vista that greeted my eye was rich with wonders. I was amongst the animals of my imagination and television viewing, and I loved it. My heart feasted from hyenas in pairs and lions in prides to herds of elephants and lone, graceful giraffes. My eyes cried at the sheer beauty of them and the disbelief that I was there with them.

We then travelled through the Great Rift Valley to Lake Naivasha to see the magnificence of the birds that called that expanse of water home. There I had my first, albeit distant, encounter with hippos. Still and silent, I sat on a rock by the edge of the water and watched them bathe. This is where David had his not-so-distant encounter with a lion when it sauntered past him as he sat out on the back porch while reading. I came out of the shower to see David scream (in a manly way, of course) and run back into the safety of the room while the lion ran in the opposite direction from the fright of some man screaming at him.

We left Africa two weeks from our arrival with my lasting connection to the beautiful place for its bountiful wildlife and bringing peace to the memory of my scared three year old self in front of the camera. I left with a strong desire to return.

From Kenya, we flew to Nepal with a one-day stopover in Delhi. Kathmandu was a cacophony of noise, colour, and smells. We wandered from the serenity of temples to the buzz of the streets and approaches of "Tiger balm," "Change money," "Hashish," all offered in fast repetition by gentle-faced boys.

From Kathmandu, we did a short river trip that included white-water rafting. The rush of the water and the joy of the group in our raft were intoxicating and filled my senses with the excitement of noise and movement. Suddenly, at one point, there were silence and darkness and a sensation of being pulled down. It felt like time had slowed down, the babble of water was gone, the chatter of people was gone, and the clarity of daylight was gone. I kept moving down for what seemed like an eternity. Slow realization—the boat had collapsed and I was in the water.

Oddly, I felt no fear. I felt very peaceful and started to quite enjoy the serenity. And then, with a sound like rushing wind in my ears, I was spat onto the surface of the river a short way from the raft. Travelling is full of great stories the journeyer loves to tell and embellish with each recounting. My embellish was to sing the theme tune from the television series *Hawaii Five-O,* as this was the last thing I had heard the boys at the front of the raft belting out as I hit the water.

From our rafting trip, we went to Chitwan National Park and amongst other activities went rhino spotting on elephant back. We did not see the illusive Nepalese black rhino, but the delight I got sitting on the back of that slow, swaying animal filled me with ample joy. It was hard for me to believe that I had gone from seeing elephants in childhood on the television to seeing them at close range in Africa, and I was now on the back of one.

We travelled from Chitwan to Pokhara, where we organized a guide, Min, to take us on a seven-day trek in the Himalayas. We followed a reasonably gentle trek of seven days as opposed to the much tougher two—or even three-month treks. However, it still involved five to six hours of trekking at an altitude of over 10,000 feet and a constant pace uphill and downhill. The scenery was magnificent, and watching the sun rise and set over snow-topped Himalayan Mountains was like a soothing balm for the eyes and soul. I loved the rhythm of life on this short trek that started with the rising sun and went to bed with it dipping behind the mountains. The domestic comforts I was so conditioned to were absent from every home. It struck me how we blindly take for granted the fact that we have hot running water, let alone the technology that we are continuously plugged into. The absence of these Western staples allowed me to appreciate the simplicity of life. The beauty and serenity of these mountains seemed etched into the spirit of every Nepalese person we met.

From the tranquillity and splendour of the Himalayan Mountains, we headed to Thailand.

After a few hot, busy days in Bangkok, we headed to northern Thailand. From the city of Chiang Mai, we went on a jungle trek. We stayed in the homes of the hill tribes and travelled by foot, elephant, and bamboo raft. The trek through the jungle was not physically demanding, but the challenge came from the heat and the lack of amenities. Despite my comfortable upbringing, I quickly adapted to the conditions easily and became quite adept at finding the perfect river rock to wash my clothes upon. And rather than crave my creature comforts, I revelled in the lack of them. I felt light and free and became very "mother earth."

After our trek, we hired a motorbike and explored the towns and villages of the north-west close to the border of Burma, choosing to head off the main roads. This motorbike adventure became one of my most treasured times travelling, because we saw no other tourists and spent hours in conversation with the local people. The happiness I felt during these days was a new sensation for me. It had a peaceful quality of "just being."

From northern Thailand, we made our way by bus and train back to Bangkok and on to the south and the island of Koi Samui. I did not enjoy this short stay, as I found it too mainstream for my free-spirited and salt-of-the-earth tastes. I was enamoured by the "road less travelled" and discovered that I am definitely an off-the-beaten-track kind of gal!

I was relieved to leave for Penang, an island half a mile off the west coast of Malaysia. We stayed in Georgetown, exploring this tiny island in one day by motorbike. I loved the decaying colonial architecture of the city, the streets filled with vendors, and the bustle of the Chinese medicine shops as cures were tipped out of jars onto brass scales and bills were reckoned on abacuses. The distinctive character and beauty of places of worship peppered Georgetown: Buddhist temples, Christian churches and cathedrals, Islamic mosques, and Hindu temples.

From Georgetown, we travelled across the Malay Peninsula to Kota Bahru on the east coast. It was very relaxing passing through the central highlands of Malaysia.

For the next ten days, we travelled slowly by bus down the east coast, stopping overnight at some of the small towns and villages. Our senses were entertained by the theatre of the local markets, with act upon act of fabrics, spices, vegetables, and fruits. We left the mainland for a three-day stopover on the island of Pulau Kapas, where home was a wooden bungalow on the beach. There were only seven other people on the island.

My time was spent in silent worship of the fish and coral life that I spent hour after solitary hour snorkelling over. My eyes drank in the wonderful, watery world I floated over as I tried to grapple with the reality of it all. I was no longer that little girl in Belfast who spent hours mesmerised by the marine natural-history programs on television. I was now swimming as a woman amidst these aquatic friends.

From the east coast, we travelled to Kuala Lumpur (KL). I found KL to be a beautiful city with a fascinating blend of old and new that did not clash but enhanced the beauty of each other. It was city that seemed to be spacious but compact at the same time.

After KL, we headed south to the amazing town of Malaka. During its history, it had been under the control of the Malay sultans; Sudanese kings; and Portuguese, Dutch, and British colonists who introduced Indian and Chinese labour and traders.

Each of these influences is evident in the architecture, place names, cuisine, and features of the local people. I loved this jigsaw of history and was content to simply wander her streets, viewing each historical piece.

From Malaysia was a short stopover in Singapore. It was a city in total contrast to the basic amenities of Nepal and the north of Thailand. I appreciated the hot, running water and clean, comfortable bed, but after four days, I was ready to leave and would have happily swapped this comfortable sojourn for even one more day in the Himalayan air or Thai jungle.

The last leg of our journey was approaching, and we were to spend the final weeks in Indonesia. As an archipelago of some 18,000 islands, we restricted ourselves to just five of them.

We flew into Medan in Sumatra to begin our three-week stay. Out first stop was the town of Brastaggi, which was high in the central mountains of the north. The skyline was dominated by an active volcano, Mount Sibayak, towering some 2,000 feet above the town. Its peak was constantly wreathed by a circle of steam. We spent an amazing day walking to the summit—the sight, hissing sound, and smell of sulphur lodging in our nostrils for days to follow. The tourist eyes in me, attracted to the strangeness of the first volcano I had ever walked on, were not blind to the presence of the local people. I watched them hunched over while harvesting the sulphur deposits, and I knew what this form of labour would be doing to their lungs. It was not the first time on my travels that I was I aware of the random nature of my birth and awoke to the appreciation that I was born into the comfort of my Irish life.

We travelled from Brastaggi south through the Sumatran highlands, stopping at Lake Toba, one of the many lakes in the crater of an extinct volcano, before moving on. Bukit Tinggi was one of my favourite spots in Sumatra. It was built on a hillside with narrow, winding streets and steep, connecting staircases sewing the town together. We stayed in Bukit Tinggi and neighbouring Lake Maninjou for about ten days. The delight of this stay was the people we met, from the hotel owners to the inhabits of Lake

Maninjou who came to know us as we spent much time hanging out with them.

With just four weeks before our arrival in Australia, we left Sumatra for Java, flying into Jakarta. Our stay Jakarta was just brief enough to pick up our visas for Australia.

While there, we went through the ritual of sending word home. Back in 1990, we hadn't yet been immersed in the age of mobile phone, email, Facebook, or Twitter. Communication with our loved ones meant writing letters and queuing at a telephone exchange in the major cities we visited. I loved calculating the different time zones, the anticipation of waiting in the queue, and then the crackly voice of my parents on the other end of the line. This ritual seemed to emphasise the sense that we were travelling far from home.

One time I called Ireland from Jakarta was daytime, and my mother was at work in her role as a telephonist. As my voice echoed back to me, "Mammy, it's Mary Jo". I heard her say to her work colleagues, "It's our Mary Jo from Jakarta."

I still smile at the simple beauty of this moment when I recall this memory. Her words oozed with pride and excitement at hearing my voice. I felt somewhat exotic, as if I belonged to some colourful place and was living a glamorous life.

Perhaps to my mother and her colleagues, I was. Perhaps these phone calls I made and letters I sent transported my mother away from Belfast to be with me. Perhaps the phone calls were more than an act of communication with her daughter. Perhaps they gave meaning to all the hours she had laboured, meaning to the many personal sacrifices she had made. I hope so.

With our visas stamped for entry into Australia, we set out on our journey around Java, stopping first in Cirebon. It was a town famed for its batik and very few tourists. I loved the array of fabric and colour that delighted my eyes and put a small hole in my wallet. I made purchase after purchase of sarongs that went to various parts of the world as presents to family and friends. Well over twenty years later some still adorn my dining table.

We then travelled to Malang, a hill town in the east where we hoped to climb Mount Bromo. However, I discovered that I had a strong allergic reaction to mosquito bites when a bite on my lower leg became swollen and blistered to half the size of my calf. My suppurated calf caused great discussion amongst the local people, and after making my way to the local hospital, it enjoyed the fame even more.

I was well looked after. Despite not sharing a spoken language with these people, I was in the presence of the universal connection of humanity, through their care and nurturing.

From Malang, we went to Yogyakarta. Our couple of days sightseeing included a visit to Borobodur, a spectacular eighth-century temple. As I walked up the staircase that led to the main temple structure, a quietness slowly moved through me with each footfall. The cone-shaped stupas, the elaborate carvings, and the weathered grey of the stone soothed me. I felt at peace despite the presence of other visitors. I found it curious that I did not feel this connection to all the temples or places of sacred worship I visited. I noticed that, more often than not, it was not the elaborate temples of wealth that brought me peace. It was the jungle-eaten or time-sculpted sacred places that spoke to me and made me feel the same as when I would walk on my beloved Cave Hill or other parts of Ireland.

We returned from Yogyakarta to catch a flight to Lombok, the last destination before we headed to Australia. For fourteen very relaxing days, we swam, snorkelled, and made great friendships with the people we met. We spent most of our time on Gilli Air, a tiny island just off the mainland. Its distance was measured by the fact it took us two hours to walk around it at a very comfortable pace.

For the first time on my travels, I seriously considered forgoing the lifestyle I was familiar with and staying put, rather than heading to Australia. Fate had other plans. David's logical argument won the day.

In March 1991, we stepped aboard the aeroplane and flew to Sydney, Australia.

This phase in my life of travelling ended with heaps of dinner-table stories to tell, great memories that would last forever, and finding the ever expanding existence of love in my life. My love for the land now stretched beyond Ireland to that of other countries. My awe-filled love of the beauty of nature multiplied, and my love for my chosen life partner deepened. Love does indeed move in mysterious and wonderful ways. We just have to be open to receive it.

Chapter 5

Life South of the Equator

Stepped off the plane in Sydney with a rucksack full of dirty clothes and an empty bank account. Despite that, I had a heart full of excitement, and my head was swimming with the possibilities of my new life in Australia. After a short stay with David's cousin, we rented a house in the inner west suburb of Annandale. We sparsely adorned it with inexpensive or second-hand furniture, makeshift bookshelves made from bricks and planks of wood, and a clothes rack for a wardrobe.

I loved our first home in Sydney. It was handy to local shops and restaurants, walking distance from my work, and a bus ride into the city. We frequented the local pizzeria and became well known by the owners. We learnt to be thrifty by going to Stanmore Cinema every week on Tuesday, as it was cheap-ticket night. Our most prized possession was a book called *Sydney by Foot and by Ferry*. At weekends, we would pick a different route and head off to explore the city we had chosen to make home. While we still had the weekly routine of work and domestic life, it also felt like we were on a working holiday, as we had so much to explore and enjoy about this beautiful city. Sometimes at the weekends, we would go farther afield and head into the Blue Mountains or along the coast.

Through work, our social life expanded, so peppered with sightseeing were invites to dinners and parties. My brother and his wife moved to Sydney in mid 1992, so with family, friends, and work colleagues in my life, I began to settle into a comfortable rhythm of life. David worked in the corporate world as a financial controller, and he thrived. He fully embraced his new working life, and between travelling for work and studying at night, he found fulfilment. I loved to see him so content, and he seemed to be the happiest I had ever known him be.

I found a job with a large, non-government organization as a sexual assault counsellor for children. From an unsure beginning with the newness of the work, I grew to love it deeply. I remember the interview clearly, especially the moment when they asked me how I felt about working for a Catholic organization. I leant slightly forward in my chair, towards the interview panel of three, and said with a wink, "Depends how Catholic you are." As I rose to leave the interview, I berated myself: *Who does that? Who gets sassy during a job interview?* I have always loved the mischievous side of my character and enjoy the ease with which my cheekiness flows in my social life, but I questioned the timing of it in the interview.

I asked one of the members of the interview panel many years later about that moment and why they would have hired me. She said it was because of my "obvious intelligence and humour." So it seemed that these two gifts were evident in my work before I could appreciate them for myself.

I loved my work as a children's counsellor, and I found I had a natural flair for it, but I also worked hard at developing my skills. When I was a child, I thought that there was a clear moment when I would "grow up" and become an adult. We mark our passage through milestones, such as the right to vote, obtaining a driving license, reaching the legal age to drink alcohol, and our first sexual experiences.

There is no such event as growing up. Instead, I discovered that I am constantly growing into my life. The knowledge of that filled me with excitement about the possibility of what I could do with my life but also brought into sharp focus those parts of myself I did not like. I struggled with trying to integrate the two. Upon reflection, the growing pains of adolescence paled into insignificance compared to the growth of my soul.

As I was thriving in my professional life and carving out a well-respected identity, that strange little girl in me who had spiritual aspirations and felt the life flow in trees and mountains stayed quiet. There was no room for her in the clinical arena. I noticed that no other well-respected professional spoke of the divine power of nature or the wisdom gained from spiritual/cultural ancestry being used in therapy. So despite very positive feedback from those I worked with, both clients and colleagues, I did not feel I was fully genuine. I just did not know what this missing genuine piece was. I knew it was to do with my spiritualty. I was just not quite ready to listen to that part of my self yet. That little girl inside me had been silenced a long time ago, and I had no intention of waking her up.

In 1992, when I was thirty years old, we moved to New Zealand. The company David worked for had offered him a promotion. When he came home to discuss it with me, I instantly agreed to the move. As the words of agreement came to my lips, I heard my heart's whisper that this move would be of great significance to me. My head was not so sure. In two years we had seen very little of the Australian country. I was also enjoying my work and starting to build a good reputation in the profession. My brother, James, and his wife, Gail, had recently emigrated from Ireland to Sydney, and I was forming a good network of friends. We were really only just getting settled in Sydney, and now we were about to disrupt this by going to a country I knew nothing about, had no family or friends in, and had no work to go to. My heart, however, was so certain this was a good move to make that I gladly packed up what little possessions we had, shipped them to Auckland, and jumped on a plane for New Zealand.

Our first few weeks in Auckland were spent living in a motel until we found a house to rent. With no car, I took public transport or walked the city with my CV in my hand and visited any community or social-work agencies I found in the telephone directory. It was an intense first few weeks, selling my skills and experience in a country where no one knew of me and I knew little of its systems. I always thought being a sales rep selling a product to a company would be a tough job. Now I was trying to sell a product that was essentially myself. I felt daunted by this unusual approach to career development. I approached it with a sense of adventure, throwing myself into it with the same philosophy of hard work as I did in all my career pursuits. So when I felt twinges of disheartenment, I brought to mind how fortunate I was to have the physical ability to walk the streets, a roof over my head at the end of a day, and training and experience to make me a viable option for employment.

I had only been in the country two weeks when I got a job at the Auckland Help Foundation. In this position, I provided counselling for children and young people who had been sexually assaulted, their siblings, and non-offending parents. I was also part of the call-out team for rape victims.

Although I had done similar work in Australia, I was required by the organization to attend an orientation course. It was on this course that I was to meet some women who would awaken that spiritual side of me that I had kept away from my profession. The three women were Hine, Tilly, and Violet. We all had to introduce ourselves by describing a picture we drew.

I listened as they spoke about the connection to family, tribe, and the land. I was bemused how these women could be talking so like the Irish. As they talked further, they spoke about the spirit of the land and energy flows. I was stopped dead in my tracks—how could these women be talking so like that girl I once was? Moreover, how could they be doing this in a professional setting?

As I showed my drawing I spoke of my people and my connection to my Irish place. They told me later they were initially cautious about me, as they had never heard a white woman speak like this. Over the next months and years, I was to become deeply connected to them. We shared the wisdom of our ancestry and culture with each other.

I saw that these women had found a way to hold on to their ancestral wisdom in the professional world of social work, and I wanted to do the same. Our talks would invigorate and excite me at the prospective of expanding my work to include not just my clinical wisdom but my cultural/spiritual wisdom, and in the process, I would encourage people to tap into the great healing potential within their own ancestry.

Under the guidance of some dear Maori friends, and particularly from within the love of Hine and Bill Rauwhero, I began to tentatively acknowledge that my cultural ancestry and my way of being in the world had some part to play in my professional voice.

I was no less of a social worker for allowing this voice to be heard. I was to turn my heart once more to my country of birth and the Irish people to find the piece that was missing for me in a way that no clinical, professional knowledge could fill. My missing piece was me and my Irish ancestry. I just had to discover how to use this service of others in my work.

From the community organization of the Help Foundation, I went to work for a government organization called the New Zealand Children and Young Persons Services (NZCYPS). The primary function of the NZCYPS is to work with families to protect children, manage young offenders, and ensure the care and security of children in need. I worked at the specialist services unit, where my role was to provide professional expertise in the assessment of children, young persons, and their families. I also provided counselling and therapy for the clients of the C&YP service referred by C&YP service social workers.

The years in New Zealand were a spiritual oasis for me. I saw that the connection I have to land and divine presence is not because I am weird but because I am Irish and have a Celtic spirit. This connection held within it the possibility that I no longer had to feel alone, different, or out of step with myself. I could now turn to the wisdom of Celtic spirituality that saw wisdom in the land and nature. I always have seen that the patterns and movement of nature constantly tell me of the need for balance, that there are times for life and times for death, times for growth and times for rest, and times for rain and times for sun. This was the wisdom of the girl who heard the heartbeat in the Celtic landscape.

This wonderful time of my awakening to the spiritual context of my professional life also coincided with the birth of my first son. My pregnancy was filled with good health and joyful anticipation of meeting this life that I felt growing inside me daily. Being pregnant also seemed to open a portal into the spiritual realm that allowed me to feel closer to my grandmother and godmother than I had ever felt before. It also sent me the presence of some Maori elders.

On more than one occasion, I would awake from sleep to see the figures of Maori older men and women standing by my bed. Once late on in my pregnancy, I awoke from an afternoon sleep to find the entire circumference of my bed encircled with Maori elders looking over me. I called Bill and Hine. As Bill answered the phone, I found myself telling him to ask his "crowd not to be so concerned about me and not send a cast of thousands to look over me." As I hung up, having chatted to him for a while, I was aware that we had had a conversation about his spiritual family visiting me in the same ordinariness of having a conversation about his living family visiting me. I cannot tell you how good that feels to be so ordinary with people rather than being worried about being strange.

Cadhla seemed very comfortable in his resting place in my body, so it took him eighteen days past his due date to come into the world. As I had chosen to have a home birth, Cadhla came into the world in our bedroom. I went to find Cadhla deep inside me. I felt myself leave the room and moving upwards into the most beautiful blue ether I have ever seen. I had never seen that colour of blue before, or since. It pulsated with a vibrant energy, and there in the middle of this blue energy field lay the curved outline of Cadhla's golden spirit. He greeted me with a familiarity and said, "I have been waiting for you for a long time," and then he started to move towards earth. I found it so peaceful that, for a split second, I wanted to stay, but I knew I had my duty as his mother to perform. At that thought and the sound of a fast-rushing wind, I was pulled back to the bedroom.

When I opened my eyes, I saw my beautiful son being held upside down by the midwife who skilfully uncurled the placenta from around his throat and placed the wrinkly, wet bundle on my chest. Then I picked up a strange scent in the room and I felt puzzled that I should be picking up the smell of fear. I was not frightened, so why was I picking up this scent? I was at peace, happy with the weight of my baby on my chest. As the feeling of peace increased, I started to become distant again from my body and surroundings. I was slowly returning to the place of vibrating blue. Before I went I wanted to tell everyone not to worry, not to be afraid, but I was too weak to form the words in my mouth. I heard someone say that I was losing too much blood as a nurse injected me on the leg, and then the gentle dark of sleep descended.

Cadhla was born in the early hours of the morning, but it was not until early afternoon of the following day that I awoke to find him sleeping peacefully beside me and someone bending over me. I could feel the gentle breeze of breath across my face. I looked into the face of a tall Maori elder in full ceremonial regalia. He looked at me with a strong but loving gaze and said, before disappearing, "You'll be right, girl." When David came to my side later, he assured me that no one had been in or out of my bedroom all day.

My blood loss was so severe it was touch and go as to whether I would be admitted to the hospital for a blood transfusion. However, this did not eventuate, and my weakened body lay in bed for several days with my only real physical ability being to drag myself up onto pillows to breastfeed my son. I would watch as he was taken from my breast by David to be washed and dressed, but at least I got to watch.

David eventually had to return to work, so I willed my body to eat iron-packed foods and to get better. By the time he left for his first day of work, I was on my feet, not sturdy but at least standing and moving around the house and venturing out on short trips that did not overtire me.

The next weeks were an arduous struggle of adjusting to young motherhood. I was extremely weakened by the physical trauma of the birth. Cadhla was in pain from gastric reflux, and I had no familial help. I was able to take some enjoyment from the beauty of my son, but this was compromised by my dread at the sheer exertion it was taking me to see the day through. It was not the emotional or even practical labour of mothering that caused me this dismay; it was being in a tired, weak, almost lifeless body that alarmed me. I felt I rose at the beginning of the day with a weight inside me and all around my physical self, and I ended the day this way but weaker.

The weeks moved into months, and when I felt myself not getting better, I could stand it no longer. I got on an aeroplane and returned to Ireland. I let everyone know this was not a holiday; this was a time of recovery. And so it was. Under the loving care of my mother, back on Irish land, I quickly returned to my body. When I flew back to New Zealand, I felt I flew back as Mary Jo.

It may have taken several months from the birth of Cadhla, but a return to happiness came into my life, and the rest of that year was spent in absolute bliss with being a mother. I felt as if I had something to give him now. I was fully engaged in my mothering, not just going through the mechanics of tasks. I delighted in every minute of getting to know the blossoming life that was my son. We played together, explored Auckland together, and got to know each other. He was great company then and still is today. Family life moved into a harmonious routine of play and nurturing and three coming together as one family.

But the peace that was my life was short lived. Just over a year from Cadhla's birth, David returned home from work to say that the company was being downsized and, as a result, his department had been reduced and he was made redundant. He worked in some temporary positions for a few months but was ill contented and wanted to return to Australia, as he felt there were better employment opportunities for him. I wanted to stay in New Zealand. We had our beautiful son, I had strengthened my connections with a group of friends, and I still had a good professional reputation. While I wanted to stay at home and care for Cadhla full time, I could return to work if we needed our income increased. I saw no need to return to Australia.

I experienced the beginning of a fundamental change in David from that time. It felt to me like there was less room in his internal landscape for us as a family and more focus on himself. He would not listen to all the bounties we had in New Zealand or my desire to stay. I had adapted my life to his career change to come to New Zealand. I now wanted what was best for the family. However, in late 1995, I found myself seated beside him on an airplane returning to Australia.

I left behind a lot: my dear friends, the family I had found in Bill and Hine, my connection to the land, my spirituality awakening, and my lovely little home. I now wonder if some of my love for David got left behind as well.

When Cadhla was born, Bill and Hine had asked if they could bestow Tama, a Maori name, on Cadhla in honour of our connection. In addition, they buried our placenta on the Maere and planted his Kofi tree on top. It was not until several years later on a return trip to New Zealand that I was able to sit under that tree and feel the depth of the past sorrow of the difficulty around my son's birth and the present grieving for my loss of New Zealand. When I left Ireland all those years ago, I remember having the physical sensation of a part of my heart breaking away and remaining there. The day I left Auckland, another piece of my heart stayed behind, perhaps buried there on the sacred land overlooking Manachu Harbour.

Chapter 6

Why Do I Love You?

When I returned to Australia, I found the perfect balance that allowed me to continue to enjoy being a mother to my son and do contract work from home. I was engaged by government and community organizations to write training manuals and consult on child protection and trauma matters. This afforded me the opportunity to be a full time mother, contribute to my profession and keep abreast of all the research and practice developments.

Life also settled into a commonplace routine of family life. I reconnected with some of the women I had met before I left for New Zealand. They had also had children. I connected with new women through meeting them at parks and children's functions and so started a whole new chapter in the life of my relationships. In becoming a mother, I belonged to this matriarchal group and loved the shared child rearing that was to unfold for many years to come.

At the beginning of 1996, I was pregnant with my second son, Conor, who came into the world in October of that year. His arrival was vastly different from that of Cadhla. When we arrived at the birthing centre at the hospital, David dropped me at the entrance to make the short journey to the front door while he quickly parked the car. As my foot hit the pavement, I had an uncontrollable urge to laugh, which I easily gave into. As I walked into the birthing centre to the midwife, the laughter was subdued only in its volume, not its intensity.

I had planned a natural birth. It was to be quiet with oils burning, gentle music, and perhaps even a water birth, as well as a girlfriend to assist. But that was not to be. I entered the birthing room laughing, the midwife shouted to David to get in the room quickly or he would miss the birth of his child, and my girlfriend never did get to attend.

Quickly and unexpectedly as the whole process was, when Conor was lifted into my arms, I gasped at the angelic quality of his beauty and the peaceful radiance that came off him. He was the most beautiful little creation I had ever seen. I told the midwife that I did not think he was here on earth yet and perhaps was still in Tir na nOg.[4] Her puzzled look told me that she thought, looking at the baby in my arms, that he was indeed here.

So here were my two sons in the world with me, and I knew that this was meant to be. Their passages here were very different, as well as their looks and their mannerisms, but each had a special quality for me. Through motherhood, I had discovered another form of sacred love, the like I had never felt before and the quality of which nothing on this world could diminish.

Because David worked long hours and studied when the boys were young, I spent many days enjoying adventures and gentle mayhem with them. I remember once having a play day which involved first a flour fight, then a water fight, and then a visit to the local café for our favourite sausage rolls and pastries. What I did not think through before our melee was that flour mixed with water made a sticky paste. Our battle-coiffured hair made all three of us look like members of a punk rock band as we scoffed our lunch greedily, satisfying the hunger born of the energy expended during our gluey skirmish.

The messiness of a life of fun was not exclusive to food fights. Often when the tooth fairy visited, she would leave a glittery trail out the bedroom door, through the house, and all the way to the garden. It was there one morning that my dear friend Terry found

---

4   Tir na nOg is one of the main spiritual realms in Irish mythology.

us on our knees, bums in the air, and we invited him to join us on the dewy grass to track her delicate footprints to her home. We never did find out where in the garden she lived.

With motherhood, my expanding heart was filled with the love of these two beautiful souls. I recognized our belonging and verbalized it in a playful catch call that resounded often in our home (and which I later wrote into a book for them).

> "Why do I love you?" "Cause you're our mama."
> "Why do I love you?" "Cause we're your boys."
> "Why do I love you?" "Cause we're so special."

Each of their responses was louder than the one before, and the beam of their smiles increased in radiance with each reply.

I felt a connection to them that went beyond the sharing of the physical form of humanity or genetic material of familial tie. We spoke of not only playthings and the unrecognised advantage of eating vegetables but also about spiritual matters and the angels that used to visit them in early childhood.

At that time in my life, I did not hear many people speak about their relationship with their children in that way. I was acutely aware of negative viewpoints about mothers and sons. I was warned not to become enmeshed with my sons as I would, as one teacher told me, be emasculating them by the way I parented. So I self-censored and told only a few close confidants of my deep spiritual love for my sons and a sense of being a guardian on their spiritual journey. I was more than a mother figure.

Seeing my maternal role as one of a guardian was to have major implications for how I parented them. I involved them on all the decision-making aspects of their lives; I encouraged their views of my parenting and I ensured we had rites of passages to mark their years. So on the day of each birthday, from when they were four, I would ask what right they wanted granted and what responsibility they wanted to accept. These rights and responsibilities were balanced with their development stage and increased in sophistication as they got older. So when at a young age they chose, for example, to make their beds as a responsibility or dry the dishes, I never corrected their efforts, no matter how poorly the job was done. It was the picking up of the responsibility and the effort that they put into it that were important, not the end result. That would come with maturation.

I remember Cadhla's total exhilaration when he was allowed to ride his bicycle to the end of our street and around the block. I can't remember how old he was when he asked for this right; all I remember was seeing his eager shoulders rounded over the handlebars, his little legs pedalling ferociously and the beam on his face that could supply power to the national grid with the strength of its energy.

I remember Conor lying under the "TV blanky" with me on the sofa to watch his first "big-boy movie." I can see his joyful sense of pride oozing out of every pore in his body as he snuggled in closely to me as the soundtrack for the movie heralded its beginning.

Now eighteen and sixteen years old, their attention has turned more naturally to relationships and matters outside the home, yet we still regularly connect. And while the conversations are no longer of childhood angels, they are no less significant. The beauty of this developing relationship with the boys was in sharp contrast to the context of my marital life.

I was blessed to spend a huge chunk of time with a dear girlfriend, Alison, and there is not one great moment in my life or my children's lives at that time that did not involve her and her daughter. As we watched our children play, we got to discuss all the important stuff of life together, which was mostly about the children we were watching at play. When they were in bed and we could share a glass of red wine, we continued our discussions. I laughed with her until my stomach hurt and cried with her until my heart no longer hurt.

I talked to her when my belief in myself as a mother faltered in the face of the times my tiredness made me impatient with Cadhla and Conor. I cried with her when my loneliness and my love for David was bleeding away before my very eyes.

I was also fortunate to find Yvonne to speak to. She was to become my Anam Cara (Irish term for confidante, spiritual mentor, and emotional supporter). Our conversations kept me from totally disintegrating into the mess that self-doubt and self-blame were having on me. At times I felt such a failure as a mother and wife. I could not make sense of this web of living I was caught in. My conversations with her revealed that if my emotional world seemed filled with great turmoil than my spiritual world was a place of tortured contradictions.

I missed the spiritual surety of New Zealand. I was at times angry at my spiritual ancestors for I felt they were no longer with me. I felt angry at myself for believing they existed in the first place. I swung between, denying their existence despite the sense of their presence and yearning for the deep connection to the spiritual world I knew existed.

These years in my spiritual diary would not be recorded as a time as a religious devotee. I did not meditate or read any books that fed my soul, nor did I engage in much formal prayer. This was a time of prayer as action. I cared for my children, spent time with my friends, worked hard in my counselling practice, and struggled in my marriage. All of which may not sound much like praying until you see the practice of love I had for my little family and friends. The prayer lay in doing washing, cooking, earning the money, and staying with my partner despite my doubts and the lack of love in my life. This may not be the common definition of prayer. However, if prayer is to be a form of worship, then what greater worship can there be than living life and continuing to find moments of joy in all the hard work and holding on to the belief in love when it seemed in short measure?

I cannot describe these years as the best years, as it would belittle what it was like for me. But I cannot describe them as the worst of years, because I got to mother my children and befriend wonderful women as well as continue to work in my beloved profession. Somehow, when I was busy being busy, my spiritual heart lay patiently under this mantle of busyness like a seed under the covering of snow, waiting for its moment to burst into life.

Looking back at it now, I see the gift of this time in my life: the recognition that all of life is seasonal. I learnt that it is not just the natural changing of the times of the years that we live through. We also go through bodily, emotional, and spiritual measures of time. Each one is connected to the other and needed as clearly as the cold of winter and the warmth of summer are needed to sustain this earth fully. I learnt to love and appreciate this human seasonal existence of ours.

On the work front, I was again fortunate enough to find writing work I could do from home when Conor was a baby. Eventually, when I needed to work more and more away from home, Cadhla was old enough to go to a local preschool program part time, and a young woman who was a family friend was able to look after Conor and Cadhla on the days he was not at preschool. However, when she could no longer do this, and after one or two failed attempts to find someone suitable to look after my children, my mother and father came to live in Sydney.

My mother cared for my son for a year while my father went back to Ireland after six months. I was able to work out of the house without worrying about my sons. I will be eternally grateful to my mother for looking after my children and they are eternally blessed as they got to spend time with her. This was a precious and rare occurrence due to the of distance between Ireland and Australia.

In my professional life, I found I became more and more conscious of working in a professional paradigm that made me feel increasingly uncomfortable. I still attended the training courses and read the books, but doubts about the infallibility of clinical wisdom increased. I found myself questioning the supremacy of one paradigm over all others. I saw a clinical framework that spoke with certainty about the correct manner of proceeding and seemed to discount a richness that lay outside the purely clinical approach.

My time in New Zealand, and my acknowledgement of my own pre-Christian ancestry, told me there was more. My unease at my own spiritual struggle and my disillusionment at the monoculture nature of the clinical approach in my professional lay hidden from the visible eye of my colleagues.

This unease initially meant that, while comfortable in publicly naming my practice Cara, I was tentative in owning the deep cultural-spiritual meaning behind it. I did not yet know how to fully integrate the wisdom from my cultural heritage with my social-work training. I was bereft of a language to explain this in a way that would not invite the derision of my profession. I was well aware of the discomfort in the clinical world when it came to matters of a spiritual nature. The few tentative conversations I had engaged in about the place of spiritual wisdom in our profession and the many times listening to others speak had clearly showed me that. Spiritual wisdom was marginalized in our profession at best and derided at worst. I don't think I was ready for either.

Those years when my children were young were certainly tumultuous ones, but they were deep in meaning. I learnt in those years that a stormy night does not turn to a brighter morning because we will it to do so; it will not shorten its longevity because we force it to do, and it cannot be wished out of existence because we want the dawn to come. The only way through to quiet dawn is through the night of the storm. I had no idea when dawn was to break or what would be washed ashore, or if indeed it would ever end. All I knew was that it had to be endured. All I knew was that I was fortunate to know love: to give love to and receive love from some very wonderful people in my life at that time. That was all I knew.

Chapter 7

Wrapped in Angels

In 2001, life visited upon me an experience that wrung the love that was in my ten-year-old marriage out of me, leaving a searing pain in its wake. Despite this ache in my heart, I did not leave the martial relationship. I not only believed in the sacred contract of my marriage vows, but I harboured doubts about my ability to survive on my own, guilt about the effect on my children, and criticism of my failure to keep the marriage together. I turned in silent pleas of prayer to Granny Gibson to help me through.

I asked her to send me images of angels as a reminder of her support and guidance, an anchor to get me through this storm. I surprised myself at the time (and since) with this thought, as I was not what you would call "the angel type": I had left the iconic behind when I left the structural confines of an organized religion. But I accepted my own quirky request and waited to accept the images of angels that my grandmother would send me. None came, despite the raging pain of my situation and my doubt in my abilities to get through it. But I did get through this difficult time intact and stronger (and without telling any of my family and friends that I was looking for angels—not something I wanted to advertise.)

Coincidently, as I came out of this difficult time some months later, I started to be sent images of angels by friends and colleagues who had no knowledge of my desire for angelic imagery. With a wry smile on my face about the timing of the late arrival of angel images, I thanked my grandmother. This was my grandmother's way of telling me that the angels were with me all the time, that they never go away. My guiding angels—my angelic hand of help through this time—were there not in image but in practice. They live in her memory and those of my godmother and aunt. They live in the beauty of nature and the sound of my favourite piece of music, and most importantly, they live in the actions of those around me who support and love me. Around my desk at work, I placed the images of angels I was sent to remember, honour, and act as symbols of being guided, protected, and strengthened in my life and in my work.

The angels did not just stay as images around my desk. They started to enter my conversations with children and young people I worked with. One such family was Tom and his mother, Chris. Tom and Chris were consulting with me one day about Tom's struggle with nightmares and being bullied at school. We spoke about his fears and doubts, his moments of triumphant, and his problem-solving skills. We also spoke about hobbies and interests, and Tom revealed his love of medieval knights: their weaponry, their armour, and their valour.

He also spoke about his aunt who had died but still guided him in many ways, and he spoke of his belief in angels.

As I listened to Tom, I heard a verse in my head that described the protection of angels. The words were originally from the breastplate of St Patrick, but I replaced the word *Christ* with *angel* and I spoke them out to him. My words flowed with natural ease like any of the healing words I spoke out in counselling, but internally I was somewhat bemused as to what I was doing voicing such non-clinical utterings.

One idea sparked off the next as we spoke of Tom's angels and breastplates that protect a knight in battle. And so Tom's shield was created with the words of the angels written on it to protect and strengthen him. He not only brought the symbolism of the shield into his waking world of the school playground but also his sleeping world: he no longer felt intimidated by the boy at school, and the monsters of his nightmares stayed away.

Through consulting with me, a young social worker called Leanne came to know of the work I did with Tom. When she left Australia to work in Ireland, she made me a magnificent tapestry upon which she had sewn the words of the angel verse. It still hangs proudly on one of the walls in the therapy centre I established some years ago now.

I remember the day that one young girl I was working with saw the tapestry. It was a day that heralded a whole new way of working and being in my life. Kay was ten. I worked with her and her foster mother on the traumatic experiences that brought her into care and the effect of these experiences on her life at that time. The first time she saw the tapestry, she asked if she could drape it around her shoulders. I told her it was a tapestry to hang on the wall, but she insisted that she be allowed to drape it upon her shoulders like a blanket. When I did, she slept for her entire session in a deep and peaceful sleep.

Due to the traumatic nature of her nightmares, sleep of this quality was a comfort that Kay did not normally enjoy. As she awoke, I told her that we would make her very own angel blanket. "What is an angel blanket?" she asked. "Well, you will have to come next week and see," I said. As she left the room, the very same question was uttered loudly by me. I had no clue of what I meant by 'Angel blanket'. I stood in the middle of my room chastising myself for saying something in a clinical context that seemed to come from no other place in my work other than out of my mouth in that moment!

I did not have to wait long to get an answer. The next day I saw what I was going to do. A week later I took Kay to the fabric store to buy a piece of fleece large enough to cover her body and some pieces of coloured cotton prints. We would then sit together and make cotton templates of all the important connections in her life—people, places, pets, events, objects, and hobbies—and sew them onto the fleece. These cotton templates represented all that sustained her and provided a source of love, comfort, joy, and support. And so I gave this blanket, and all others that have come after it, the name *angel blankets*.

I have watched over the years as needle and thread connected with fleece and stories of love and strength and fun and achievement came into multicoloured being to give meaning to experiences that were deserving of being known and honoured. I listened as children, adults, and professionals talked about the depth that angel blankets brought them to and the sheer joy of making one.

Through what I know to be divine guidance, I was inspired to develop the beautiful process of angel blankets that has allowed the spiritual-cultural nature of who I am to sit authentically alongside the clinical knowledge in my counselling work. Out of this time of pain for me came this great gift not only to my profession but also to my own spiritual healing. I marvelled at how fortunate I was to be given this guidance to develop angel blankets, how at a time of inaccessible love I was wrapped in the spiritual love of my grandmother and passed this on in my work for people to access their own unique sources of love.

As I facilitated the making of angel blankets with children, families, and adults who had experienced abuse or trauma, I watched how the freedom to share or stay silent in their work gave them mastery over their healing process rather than being a respondent to professional therapeutic questioning. I saw how the movement of needle and thread and the feel of fabric on fabric gives comfort and connection in the presence of someone who is there to hear a story if it is to be told. Sitting beside one boy and watching the movement as he put the needle into the fabric and I drew it out again connected each of us to a creativity that released some of his anguish and some of his joy. Threads of cotton connected with threads of his life as he spoke about the symbols of love and protection that he sewed onto his blanket. He spoke more freely than at any time I had tried to ask the "right" therapeutic questions.

In working with angel blankets, I find myself connected to Celtic mysticism. It is a mysticism that sees at times, rather than us going on a spiritual search, the soul discovering us in our human form, sitting or working, playing or sleeping, and it brings us comfort. It cares for us; it brings love. We do not need to seek a divine intervention or call upon a spiritual source. This love is present in us and all around us already. It was both an exalting and humbling professional experience, and I felt at peace with my professional self. In angel blanket work, I connected to the depth in being an *Anam Cara*, that part of me that is of my spiritual-cultural being, and a clinical therapist, that part of me that is of my professional training.

Close colleagues noticed this aspect of my work and encouraged me to share it with the profession. And so began a journey that took me to the point of facilitating angel blankets with other agencies outside my own practice, presenting at conferences, and eventually writing a book I named *Wrapped in Angels*. Sharing angel blankets outside the confines of my own practice gave me the opportunity to contemplate further my professional identity and to focus on how I could find the language to explain how I truly practised. I was all too aware of the experience of my work being legitimized within my profession when I described it in clinical terms but being derided if I attempted to describe it in spiritual-cultural terms. I was warned against taking my work in this direction with words that clearly suggested the shallowness of a "New Age approach" and advised I would "jeopardize my very good reputation."

The first time I publicly presented my work on angels blankets was at a conference in Canada. I was deeply moved by the honoring of my work by those who attended my workshop. This gave me the courage to think about writing and presenting the work further and permanently placed the Canadian people on a comfy armchair of love in my heart.

As life would have its way, my writing was delayed by the revisiting of the issues in my marriage that heralded in the wave of pain that preceded angel blankets. Before I was to write one more word about angel blankets, the next chapter of my life was being penned.

Chapter 8

Two Worlds Colliding

As I walked out of the dining room that Saturday morning in December 2006 into the garden, I knew my marriage of fifteen years was over. My life was about to be radically changed. So I did what any sensible person would do as they felt the approaching of an emotional storm: I hung out the washing. My arms moved mechanically from linen basket to peg basket to washing line. I distantly watched the slow, heavy movement of those arms. This leaden effort faltered only by a male voice asking me if I wanted him to leave. The thickness that surrounded my mechanical actions was finally penetrated by the rage of my words: "Not the weekend before Christmas."

We had two young children, and his words snapped me quickly out of my world and into theirs and the impact that such news would have on them. Rage filtrated into a pain that was to keep me company for a very long time. "Let's get Christmas over and give them a good time, then you can leave," were the only words I thinly spoke.

With my words still hanging around the hills hoist, I walked away from him to a far corner of the garden. I sat on my stone bench that hugged the base of a beautiful jacaranda tree—my favourite tree. A tree I planted in memory of my godmother, Kitty Gibson. Sitting there had always brought me the comfort of her memory and into the presence of those family times in my Belfast childhood. However, this time I was in the presence of a moment not from the past but in the present. I was sitting on the edge of a precipice. My heart that could barely stand the knowledge that my love had withered and died, crumbled at the thought of my sons having to endure the separation of their parents. The air around me slowed nervously, stilling itself to be witness to the moment of my breakdown.

I watched it all play out in my head: the ambulance that would bring my empty and distant body to the psychiatric wing of the local hospital, the doctors around my bed probing questions at me to break my silent responses, and the nurse's efficient hands moving me in the bed. The only part I had to play in these scenes was to make the decision that would allow the breakdown to commence. It seemed simple really, just one small decision with no fanfare, no dramatic gesture, and no irrational outburst. Just a quiet decision to mentally disintegrate. Strange as it may seem to the reader, I knew in that moment that my only part in the deterioration of my mental health was to decide to let go and let it happen.

Then the air moved with a gentle motion. I became aware of love's tender presence. The next decision I made came from within its caring embrace. I rose from the bench and returned to the washing line. The importance of the task of wet school uniforms to be hung up took the place where the decision to engage with my breakdown had sat. It was my decision to live through this stormy night, come what may, and be the mother to my children I had always been.

Once the decision was made, it felt like someone hit an accelerator button and life for the next couple of years sped up at a horrifying pace, heaping one painful situation on top of another, as relentless as any weather-created storm.

That year, the Christmas holiday went by in a blur as we attended the various festive social functions as a family. People say misery loves company, so I kept my painful secret to myself to protect the people I love from my misery. I heard myself scream as loudly in anguish on the inside as I as was silent on the outside. Each smile caused the knot in my stomach to tighten, every response of "I'm fine" deepened the invisible gash in my chest, but I did it—for my children, my family, my friends, and myself. I told myself everything would be fine if I could just get through this time.

I share the dreams of many who grow into adulthood. The ordinary stuff of life—parenting, home, paid employment—I enjoy. I had long dreamed of and worked hard for a home to shelter my children in. A home I could share with the person I would love for life. These dreams were ripped savagely from my heart.

Soon after the separation I uncovered major unpaid bills and debt into the thousands. The bank contacted me to tell me that it was only a matter of weeks before it was foreclosing on the mortgage. Despite my pleas for help to keep a roof over my sons head the disembodied voice told me he had heard it all before. There was no reprieve. We would lose our family home. As I heard the click of the replaced receiver on the other end of the phone, my body folded. I lay on the bed, crumpled body on crumpled sheets. To "get back on my feet," I had to get back on my feet, so I got up from the bed.

My two young children had only months before suffered the loss of the familiar family structure. I did not want them to endure any further pain. So I sat them in front of the television to watch a DVD. They thought all their birthdays had come at once. It was a school night, and they had ice cream and a DVD.

I had to find enough money to reduce this debt—what did I have that could make me this amount of money? I had my skills to sell. I rang several people in the profession to see if they had any extra work. Pam, Cathy, and Leonie came to my rescue with training contracts. I arranged with the bank to pay off the debt in instalments. Several months and many long hours of work later, I managed to do so, but at great personal cost that left my health compromised, my spirit worn out, and my heart completely empty from exertion. So with great emotional difficulty, I put our beautiful home up for sale.

This physical place of bricks and mortar was to be the spiritual nest from which I would nurture my two children. I wanted love to fill every room and have this energy embrace my sons each day when they returned home from school, each moment when they ran around it and slept under its roof. Many people appreciate the sanctity of a place of religious worship; I wanted a home for my children that would be their sacred ground, and now it was going.

On the morning of the first house viewing by expectant vendors, my friend, Louise, came early to ensure I got out of the house before my distress was multiplied by seeing them arriving. She stood near me as I gripped the wooden kitchen table tightly, thinking nothing as my mind was fogged by the bodily pain of loss. I do not know how I let go. But let go I did without looking back at her I walked out the front door and to the home of another friend. Richard opened the front door, and in the strength of his silence, I walked along the length of their home, into their bedroom, and into the arms of my friend, Alison.

It was a ritual we three were to perform many times in the coming months.

Despite being wearied by loss and worn by the relentless anger directed at me by David I still had to function as a mother and a professional. The physical weight dropped off me in an alarming way to reveal a haggard, sleep-deprived frame. I felt ghost-like; joy seemed in sort measure and a far-distant experience.

When my eleven-year-old son came home from school and for the first time saw the SOLD sign across the billboard that the real estate agent had erected, he sobbed. His little body broke into my arms. I called the Real Estate company. It was removed the day after my call. My son did not have to endure the visual reminder of his loss. Perhaps he too shared my dream of his home as sacred place of rest and his tears were the acknowledgment of its loss.

On my last visit to our home, as I closed the front door behind me, I screamed loudly, filling up the emptiness of the rooms with my disappointment. I swore at the cards life had dealt me. Through shouts and swears came my screeching question. WHY were all my dreams, was being cruelly taken from me. No answer. Only silence and the house flinching from the force of my anger.

As difficult as the loss of the home and the impact of waves of David's anger crashing all over me, nothing—but nothing—compared to those first weekends without my children.

I did not feel as if someone had ripped my heart out. I knew that they had, and every one of my major organs with it. I do not know how life will measure me or write the eternal story of who I was. I do know this story, will show that the most beautiful gifts I have ever been given are my two children. Of all love I have carried into this world, the love for them fills me with the greatest purpose and the perfect sense of knowing what I was always meant to be their mother.

As natural and effortless as breathing is loving them. It never occurred to me that I would not be able to practise this love full time until they were ready to leave home in their own allotted time. Nothing could have prepared me for the pain of not parenting them full time due to the practical circumstances of the separation.

There was no question that they would have an ongoing relationship with both me and their father and that we would be fully in their lives despite not living under the same roof. My pain does not relate to custody issues; it relates to the raw grief of loss. I remember that very first Friday night when I arrived home to the cold darkness of an empty home. I got as far as the kitchen and moved no farther. The pain so acute that my body's natural reflex action took over and I found myself curled up in a tight ball on the floor. I cried until the dry sobs that rose from my throat sounded like the shriek of a snared animal.

I am not sure how long it took until I heard a faint knock on my front door. I was in no fit state to see anyone, so I lay there refusing to answer it; for all I cared, the world could go on around me. I did not want to be a part of it. The knock came again, so I reluctantly rose to answer the door. There on my front doorstep was my dear friend and next-door neighbour, Mary Anne, with a pasta dinner and bottle of red wine. She did not pressure me to come next door to eat or chat with her long on the doorstep. She knew what I needed: food and to be alone.

Two weeks later, I could be found on another Friday night lying in my bed this time and again crying. I decided not to go to the school function I had bought a ticket for. It would have been too overwhelming for me to walk in alone to that large room full of all those people talking and dancing. So once again, I lay in the cold darkness of that house. Then I heard the tenor of a soft internal voice gently encouraging me to join the school celebration. I turned my back on its urging, but it persisted with telling me to go to the school function. It told me that there was something waiting for me. I begrudgingly got out of bed, half-heartedly dressed, applied make-up and masked my diffident heart. Even as I stepped through the door, I kept telling myself that I could leave at any time.

I sat at a table of familiar faces and joined in with the conversations around me. At one point, someone asked me to dance. I obliged. The body moved in time to the music; the heart was motionless. One of the women I had gotten to know over the years that our children went to school together came up to me. She moved the top of her dress slightly to reveal a tattoo on her upper chest. I smiled as she winked. "Well done," I said, pleased that she had joined me in adorning her body with ink, as I had done for my fortieth birthday several years before.

My smile caused a little stirring in my heart. Two minutes later, another woman came up and did the same. My smile was bigger as I began to ponder that the two of them had found the joy of body art. But as the third one came up to me with bosom at the ready, the penny dropped. Cathy, Connie, Karen, and Jo, who are now known affectionately by me as "my tattooed ladies," had put removable tattoos on themselves in an effort to cheer me up. It worked. My smile erupted into tearful laughter, and my heart opened up. These four wonderful women that night showed me it was still possible for me to have fun, and that joy would return. The persistent voice that spoke to me earlier in my sorrow was right. There was something waiting for me that night at that the school function: these four great women and fun!

Childcare arrangements between David and I meant that we each had half the school holidays with the boys. During the holidays when I had the boys in my care, I would take them away somewhere. We went on several road trips through Tasmania, Queensland, and South Australia. Eventually, our travels would take us farther afield, but during these years, we had fun discovering more of their home country and what it was like for the three of us to be with each other for long stretches of time. Each time we went away seemed to be better than the one before. We discovered great joy in each other's company and became really good travelling companions.

However I dreaded the first Christmas holidays that I was to have without my young sons in my care nor be with them on Christmas day. I was showered with invites from friends to spend Christmas day with them. I did not know what would be worse for me: to spend the day alone or watch other families enjoy being together. I knew I would find Christmas day difficult, and I did not want to subject my friends to my misery or face the painful onslaught to my heart I imagined that day would bring.

I phoned my friend, Yvan who is a travel agent. With very short he made travel plans to get me out of Australia to somewhere beautiful.

A few days before Christmas, I found myself sitting on an aeroplane heading to Asia. The days prior to flying had been incredibly busy, so when I sat on the aeroplane, it was the first time I looked at my travel itinerary for Laos and Cambodia. It dawned on me that I was about to travel on my own in countries I had never been to before, without being able to speak the language. While I claim my love of travel, I never saw myself doing it alone. That was for the brave of this world; courage was not an attribute I associated with myself.

When I got into the hotel room in Vientiane, Laos, I showered and then sat on the end of the bed, pondering the rashness of my behaviour. I decided that the safest plan was to stay in the hotel for the four weeks and not venture into the city on my own or indeed travel around Laos and Cambodia.

A few minutes later, I decided to risk a walk to the end of the street and back again. As I did this, I noticed the curling corner of a temple in the near distance. My curiosity and my love of exploring took me straight to it, and then the next temple on the street map, and then straight into a small tour operator to investigate what was on offer for a lone tourist in Vientiane. Less than an hour later,

I was on the back of a motorbike with Phet, who became my guide and is now a dear friend to me and my sons.

It has been several years since that morning when I walked out of the hotel room. My feet have taken me not only to the end of the street in Vientiane but throughout Laos, Cambodia, Vietnam, Peru, Chile, Bolivia, Hawaii, and a few islands in the Pacific. I learnt that when my fear was present, courage presented itself. I renewed my love of travelling, only this time I did not have to rely on the company of someone else. I could make my own travelling dreams happen. I learnt to do all of this on my own. Those years of travelling on my own turned what was left of that timid child in me into a brave adventurer, not one who had gotten rid of all her fears but certainly not one who was to going to be pushed around by them!

At this time in my life another courage started to surface more. I was beginning to integrate the spiritual-cultural part of my being into my professional identity. It was not without struggle that I melded my personal and professional identity.

My training emphasised the importance of maintaining appropriate boundaries between the personal and professional. I liked this and supported the ethical stance my profession took. It kept the people I worked with safe in the knowledge that I was accountable to meet their therapeutic needs. It also afforded me the right to my privacy and kept relationships with my co-workers in a collegial space. I was able to maintain a belief in boundaried relationships that did not equate to absolute servitude.

By the time I had written and presented on angel blankets, I had acquired a highly regarded reputation in my profession. This mystified me, as I had never sought it. I felt it was undeserved, as I seemed to have gained it through what came with ease to me: diligence to my work, my pursuit of knowledge in service of others, my considered and ethical approach, and my absolute love of being part of someone's healing.

As much as I felt honoured to receive my colleagues' high regard, it was also a source of great discomfort to me. I wondered if people in my profession would think and speak differently of me if they knew of my struggles and my pain, if they knew that there were aspects of me as broken in heart and in need of healing as the people we work with. Separating from David brought some of these aspects of me into the profession.

I turned up to professional functions no longer with a partner, my wedding ring was no longer on my finger, the weight dropped off my body at an alarming rate, and I entered into family law court mediation circles where some may have known who I was. The words of one person in my profession highlighted to me the pressure of this repudiation. "It makes you think if Mary Jo Mc Veigh can't make a relationship work, what hope is there for the rest of us?"

My repudiation as a competent professional of high standing had somehow transported itself into personal perfection, to be a superwoman without flaws. I was under an incredible amount of personal pressure, and I felt as if my professional identity was under an incredible amount of strain. I waited for the shame of the day when I would unravel in front of the entire profession. I had to juggle so much personally and professionally that I wondered if all the balls would come crashing down around me. I dreaded the public exposure. But with so many depending on me, I could not let this happen. I felt this burden both for myself and the people who looked to me for guidance and support. It was a time of great turmoil.

The long practiced ease of keeping the two worlds separate was slipping away from me. No one in the profession had previously known of the difficulties I had gone through in my marriage. However, the public nature of divorce made that known. I white-knuckled my way through this time. I just prayed no one would realize how much pain existed in my life. I felt on the precipice of the two worlds colliding, hoping that I would not reveal the mess that this divorce had turned my life into. As I surrendered to the unfolding of my life, I saw that the narrowing gap between the two sides of my life did not end my ability to be professional or strip me of my personal dignity. I gave myself permission to be exactly who I am and live my life with no shame, if people came to know of my circumstances. I started to bring love to those parts of myself that cringed at my lack of perfection, those parts wanted to shame me for my personal struggles. I stopped resisting my circumstances. I simply responded to myself in love when those doubtful moments arose.

Two very difficult years passed. Despite my original misgivings, the pain had eased and equilibrium had settled back into the rhythm of my personal and professional life. I was still highly regarded in the profession. I was still a very competent mother, a fun friend to be with, and an intrepid adventurer. I had written the wisdom of angel blankets down and published *Wrapped in Angels*. I had expanded my sole practice to invite in other professionals so children and families could have a more comprehensive service. My children were flourishing, and we planned to buy a family home once again. After many long years before and after the disintegration of my marriage, I felt more hopeful for my children and myself.

I had enough money in my saving account to put as a deposit on a house. I was excited at the prospect of providing a permanent home again. I joyfully told a friend that I saw light at the end of the tunnel. Little did I know that all the events leading to this point were but a prelude to the seemingly impenetrable darkness that was waiting just beyond this light in my life.

I was about to face one of the greatest challenges of my life, and this time my adversity would bring me face-to-face with the fragility of my mortality.

Chapter 9

Just a Routine Check-Up

*O*n May 2007, I went for a routine medical check-up. At the end of the consultation, the doctor asked a question for which my answer caused him to recommend a colonoscopy. I remember thinking he was being a bit cautious, and I might have, in my playful way, called him a drama queen. But I acquiesced to his medical expertise and had the procedure.

On a Wednesday night in June, I answered a phone call that was to change my life dramatically. He told me I had bowel cancer. His telling had to be very forceful, because his multiple requests that I come into his consulting room the next day were fobbed off by me as I was running a training course. I was training my beloved *Wrapped in Angels* and nothing could come in the way of that until he spoke the word *cancer*. I agreed to come in but only after I had finished the training day. I felt I had an obligation to follow through on the training, and as he could see me late in the day, no one needed to be inconvenienced by this news. I also went home and looked after my boys as if no phone call had been made.

A colleague took me to the consulting room of the surgical specialist on the Thursday afternoon. I was shown diagrams of the human body and how much was to be cut out of mine. I was given information on possible outcomes for me, from having a colostomy bag to chemotherapy. I could feel a thin wafer presence of my death in the room, but it was not spoken of. It did not seem to be a considered option. A cascade of emotions from a spontaneous outpouring of humour to anger that I could not go home to Ireland for a family gathering poured out of me during that appointment. Yet I recall mostly the humour that seemed to come with ease as I talked to him. I recall the doctor having to stop writing his clinical notes at one point because he was laughing too much at my humorous ponderings of, amongst other things, the "bag." Having been told I may have to live with a colostomy bag temporarily or permanently, I voiced my doubts that we weren't talking "Gucci" and I would not get shoes to match. After all, life-threatening diseases are no excuse for poor fashion sense.

I have been sagely told by several in my profession, on recounting this story, that I obviously used humour either as a survival technique or as a mechanism of denial in the face of traumatic news. I am curious about the ease with which some people can, while listening to a person's deeply personal experience, feel entitled to speak such commonly dispensed wisdom. This was not a time to tell me what I was or wasn't doing. It was the time to listen.

I was not offended when people spoke about me like that. I just knew it was totally inaccurate and dismissive of my experience. The humour was not forced or used to hide behind. There was no way for me to get away from the horror of the news I had just received, nor did I contemplate doing so. My thoughts were about facing this horror with as little pain to my children, inconvenience to my family and friends, and disruption to my clients and colleagues as possible. The humour, along with all my other reactions, came from a pure spontaneous source. This is just who I am. It is also a trait of being Irish. It has been said of us Irish that what some people don't understand is that we can be as capable of serious thought as anyone can, but we just do it with a smile.

Telling my sons I had cancer was an experience that nothing could prepare me for, not my social-work training, not words of wisdom from others, and not all the medical information from the doctors about bowel cancer. So I did it the only way I knew how. From a deep wellspring of love for Cadhla and Conor, I found the words to tell them.

I first took time to nestle all my own reactions within the comfort of my soul. I did not have to deny to myself my own emotions or swamp my children with their intensity. This "self-and-them" care allowed me to focus on them. They were, my main priority from the time I was told about the cancer.

I tended to the practical elements first so that everything was in place for their care before I spoke to them. This ensured that they would know exactly what was to happen for them when I was in the hospital and when I returned home. I translated the medical talk into Cadhla-Conor talk and repeated it the week before I went into the hospital, revealing more information each time so they could digest it all in bite-size pieces. I encouraged them to ask as many questions as they wanted and answered as honestly as I could, even if that meant saying I did not know the answer. And then I spent time talking about what it is like and what they needed while they lived with some of this unknown.

I decided, until I knew my prognosis, I would not use the word *cancer*. Their entire knowledge of cancer was as a bringer of death. They always saw their mama as the strong one, the one who knew what to do, how to solve all problems, how to bring comfort, and how to laugh while doing it! I felt they had enough to absorb. I knew that the news that I was going into the hospital would cause them alarm and lead them to question my mortality, so I chose not to bring the harbinger of death—cancer—into the picture at this stage. That was a conversation we had after I was told I was cancer free and they were able to purge all their fears about my dying.

I tried hard to do the best by my two boys, but then I did what I would describe as falling at the last post. On what should have been my last night with them, my colleagues at my practice asked for a meeting to discuss work matters. I was reassured it would not last beyond a certain time. However, as work events go, it did, and I did not take my children out for the pizza meal they so love. I lived with that regret long after cancer had left my body. That evening represented for me the trap that had formed around my identity. I was pulled and pushed between personal and professional responsibilities. Like all professionals, I had been juggling both all my working life, but in the week preceding my hospitalization, I was wading laboriously through a treacle of it! Advice came from all directions about my responsibilities in both my worlds.

> "You should only tell clients this much."
> "You need to put yourself first."
> "You should tell clients everything."
> "You should put your children first."

And although I worked diligently that week and achieved almost everything I wanted to in terms of easing the difficulties for my children, preparing my clients, and fully briefing my colleagues, I harboured doubts as to whether I had cared for everyone adequately enough. These doubts were the predecessors of much worse self-doubt to come. Logic is a useless friend in these moments. I knew I did not cause myself to have cancer, but when I saw the worry and sadness on their faces, I felt I was the source of it.

The last few days preceding admission to the hospital were filled with medical appointments and discussions with admission doctors, anaesthetists, and hospital social workers. I attended all these appointment on my own. This bureaucratic maze of procedures I navigated through kept my focus away from my aloneness and the cancerous presence in my body.

The night before I was admitted into hospital, the boys were staying with their father. I made a few quick phone calls, had a brief visit from one of my colleagues, and then spent the evening with the phone unplugged, no television, and no music playing as I moved silently through the house, making sure all was ready for my sister to look after my sons. I had the freezer and fridge filled with food, their beds with fresh linen, and the house clean. It was my choice to perform acts of mothering rather than be in the company of others. It was what I wanted to do.

When I got up the next morning, I prepared myself to be admitted to the hospital. I felt weakened by the twenty-four-hour fast in preparation for my operation. I felt uncertain as to what was to happen, as I had never spent a day in the hospital my forty-five years. I felt bereft of my ability to hug my children. To reassure and comfort them through this most difficult of times.

After some time in silent prayer, I finally closed the door behind me and allowed my spiritual mentor, Yvonne, and my friend, Mary Anne, to bring me to the hospital. They stayed until I was finally brought into the preoperating room. I was blessed to have them by my side. All was calm inside me until the moment they left and I lay flat on the bed and then was wheeled down the corridor, the moving ceilings, bright lights, and hospital noises my only companions. I felt vulnerable, and my crying began.

The crying did not emerge from me as an adult woman, competent mother, and a highly skilled professional. It felt like it came from a vulnerable, bewildered, little girl who could find no arms to fall into for comfort. This vulnerable me was wheeled into the operating theatre to be in the presence of competent, fully functioning professionals who chatted freely and with ease in a room sharp with steel, lights, cleanliness. Then, darkness as they asked me to count, one, two, thr . . .

I awoke to the feel of Alison's hand in mine, my other friend, Eric, reading to me, and tubes and beeping machines, and sense of my own physical weakness. The presence of Alison and Eric was another of my life's blessings. I surrendered to the comfort of them being near me. I drifted in and out of sleep.

Several hours later, I awoke to the semi-darkness of the ward. Alison and Eric were gone. My thoughts started to race through the last four years of my life. The nature of these thoughts was creepily mechanic in nature. It was like watching a slideshow presentation of my life from a distant. The images were orderly, and emotionless. I had little connection to this exposition. The mental presentation then jumped erratically from my past preoperative life to my immediate life in the ward. The light pressure of the oxygen mask on my face assisted my breathing; the discomfort of the tubes brought nutrients into my body and took the waste products out; the pain at the entry of the surgical wound set my entire body on edge. All of this placed me inescapably in the centre of the fragile nature of my human existence.

This weakened, flawed body was under the constant monitoring and supervision of others. Someone would perform the intimate and once taken for granted task of washing my body. Another would empty a bag of my waste products that was now attached to my stomach, a bag which would become my companion for the next months. A far cry from Gucci, darling!

My younger sister, Roisin, who lived in Sydney, was mothering my children and caring for my home. My colleagues were completing all my therapeutic, training, and consulting work. Life was functioning normally in my absence.

My mind moved from noticing my scarred and damaged physical frame to sharply focus on all the other losses I had sustained in the last two years of my life: marriage, ownership of my family home, and financial security. I lay there with no reprieve from these thoughts. I sank into a misery that goaded me about how I had been stripped of so much that society values. And now cancer had ensured that in a society that worships physical strength, youth, and perfection, I had "lesser" status. I could not even perform the most basic task of toileting myself. All I could see was that the certainty of my identity that had previously existed was now replaced with nagging doubts of who I really was: What use was I to people whom I loved? What was the measure of my value to my family, friends, profession, and society? What worth was I? I could do nothing for others or myself.

The nights taunted me.

"Who are you?"

I felt the enormity of my worthlessness.

During my time in hospital, I lived with two sides of myself. By day, I engaged in moments of humour, leant a listening ear to other patients, and engaged in playful banter with the doctors on their daily ward rounds. It lightened the gravity with which they asked me to reveal my stomach, made serious-sounding noises when they looked at the surgical incision, or seemed keenly interested in my urinating habits. But by night, it seemed darkness brought self-doubt. My own internal darkness would engulf me, and I lost connection to the vivacious, cheeky self that asked the same doctors to reveal their stomachs to me.

These nocturnal taunts drew in the external darkness of the hospital ward to merge with the internal darkness from which these thoughts were born. I spoke in my thoughts to my grandmother and my aunt and the spiritual others I felt gathered around me. I asked for their guidance and support. I asked that I live to see my sons grow to manhood. I asked, if I was to survive, that I would be granted the grace to find meaning in the pain of this experience so that I could help others. I asked for the courage to face whatever came next.

As I lay with my eyes closed and hot tears slowly and noiselessly rolling down my cheek, I felt my whole being—my body, my mind, and my spirit—slip into what felt like a river. The waters of this river were torrents of human suffering. My pain merged with generations of others from every part of the world. I felt it as clearly as I felt the tubes in my body, the oxygen mask on my face, and the scratching hospital sheets. At the time, it did not feel frightening or unusual. It just seemed like an ordinary experience for me to have. There was no fanfare of profound enlightenment, just me lying in a hospital bed and being in painful union with the whole of humanity.

The day after the operation, I had a major allergic reaction to morphine. A wave of nausea first washed through me, and then I had horrifying visions of a great source of evil surrounded by minor demons coming to claim my soul. Their screeching laughter and hunger for my soul created the most petrifying experience I have ever been through.

My chest tighten in pain. I thought I was having a heart attack and sensed my death was imminent. This confused me. I had always thought that my death would be peaceful and happy. Yet these death harbingers were causing me utter terror.

A team of doctors circled my bed. I managed to tell them of the tightness in my chest, but before I could tell them of the bigger problem of the demonic presence at the head of my bed, they locked themselves into debating what was wrong with me. My terror grew, and then a young nurse softly nudged her way through them, came to my side, and held my hand. I feebly pleaded with her not to let them take me. I was talking about the devils. I do not know what she thought I was talking about, but she gently leant towards me, promising she would let no one take me. An angel had arrived in the midst of the medical deliberation and the hellish pursuit that was going on around me. I felt safer with my hand in her hand.

After what seemed like hours for me but was in fact only minutes, a doctor told me that they felt I had an allergic reaction to the morphine and I was injected with something to counteract its effects. Within moments, my body was violently shaking, and I began to vomit. Being the day after the operation, there was nothing in my stomach to reject so the pain of the stomach convulsions across the surgery scar was excruciating. The good news was that the demons had receded back into hell.

My physical pain turned to emotional turmoil as I looked up from my spasms to see Conor at the end of the bed, his little face fastened in a grimace of utter fear. I felt a rage course through me as to how he was let in, and then I felt an overwhelming pain for him. He should never have seen his mother like this. I gestured to the nurse to get him out of the ward.

From that time, I took no opiate-based painkillers and managed my pain with the minimal help of Panadol and the strength of my own breath. I can vouch for the inability of Panadol to ease severe pain. The strength of the pain was, however, no match to my determination to get stronger for my children. So the next day before their visit, I asked the nurse to prop me up in the chair so I could be sitting up for their next visit. The day after that, I walked them to the end of my bed. The day after that, to the end of the ward. I willed my broken and sore body to move farther and farther each day so my sons would not carry the burden of what they had seen several days before.

I had to learn to manage my colostomy bag before I went home. I walked a little farther every day so I could be physically ready, and I waited for the results that the cancer had not spread to my lymph system so I could be discharged. These things gave me purpose and a small notion of my old self. But the feelings attached to them were small shards of a scattering sense of the true Mary Jo.

This disconnection was most sharply felt and cemented into my being one day when some of my colleagues from my practice came to visit me to discuss some work-related matters and in the course of doing so asked me to sign some cheques. I can still vividly recall holding the pen and slowly forming the letters of my name. I saw a look of anger on the face of my girlfriend who had popped in to see me on her lunch break. It did not register on me at the time why she would look so enraged.

To the outside observer this signing of a form may have looked like an everyday occurrence, but for me it was sheer anguish. As I held the pen, I was struggling to form the letters that I had known how to write for well over forty years. I was struggling to spell the name I was given by my family. As the ink's patterns wrote the words, I did not know the person to whom the name belonged.

The surgeon then came walking down the ward towards me with the nurse unit manager. He had never visited me in her presence before, and I knew why he was doing so now. He was going to get her to tell me the cancer had spread to my lymph system, which was how Uncle PJ had died. This was the moment I had been dreading. Through my unexpected eruption of howling tears, I was able to hear him say that the results were not back yet. He was not here to give me that news. Reprieve.

My colleagues stayed after the surgeon left. They needed to talk more about work. They needed to tell me that there was disquiet among the team about the legitimacy under which I was receiving a principal's fee. I cannot recall any of the words of that conversation, but I remember the utter despair that began to grow inside me. When they left, I took to writing a justification of my position as principal of the practice I had developed over many years and invited them into. I remember the deep sobs as I struggled to write every word, and as pen weakly scratched over the paper, the more and more unworthy I felt. Unworthiness pinned me to that hospital bed, its weight crushing my chest, and in my dismay, I searched to understand what was happening. Wasn't trying to recover from this operation and fighting the fear of death enough already? How could I stand up for myself? I felt so worthless and didn't even know who that self was anymore.

I was discharged from hospital within two days of this experience—free of lymph cancer but with a colostomy bag to manage as a result of the surgery. But struggle to find my former self did not ease when I was discharged from the hospital. It gained momentum. Despite this, I desperately clung to scraps of my former self. I reached for the motivation to keep going and found my strength once again in the warm embrace of Love.

Chapter 10

Into the Darkness

Shortly after I was discharged from the hospital, we had to leave the rental property the boys and I were living in. This had been prearranged before the diagnosis. It turned out better for us in the long run. Our new home was closer to the hospital for all my follow-up appointments, within walking distance my therapy centre, and easier for the boys to get to school. We now lived in a peaceful area and closer to local amenities.

An incredible team of friends helped with the move. In fact, they did more than help. They did the entire move for me. Shifts of people packed and unpacked boxes, cleaned, and moved furniture around. Two of my friends, Louise and Ray, came to do a stint of unpacking. Upon seeing how drained and weakened I was, Louise lovingly frog-marched us into her car to take us to their home to be cared for them until I was stronger. When the boys and I left there and finally settled into our new home life, I attempted to go back to the normality of family life. To all intents and purposes, on the surface it looked like that.

My mornings would often be heralded by a damp feeling, the acrid smell of a leaking colostomy bag, or the sight of its contents leaking on yet another set of clean sheets. I came to dread those eye-opening moments. I would then start laboriously stripping the bed, soaking the soiled sheets and nightwear, and showering. I learnt to do this all as quickly as possible to shield the boys from this stench-filled morning.

Before my diagnosis, I exercised regularly and was in strong physical condition. In the shower those mornings, I would look down at my weakened frame, my stomach displaying its scars and the internal organs hanging outside my body. My tears would join the stream of water falling from the showerhead. As I tended to the scar and cleaned the stoma to ensure both got no infections, my touch was gentle, not loving in its tenderness. I shied away from my body. It had let me down, and if I trusted in its strength or vitality again, it might fail me again. I did not want to risk the impact of this on my waning spirit. So while I washed and fed my body, I covered it in baggy clothing not only to hide the colostomy from the world but also to hide my body from myself.

Having readied myself, I would then make the boys their breakfast and pack their lunch for school. That I often locked us out of the house, lost the car keys, slept in past the alarm, or was disorganized was accepted by all three of us as our new way of being. We were very fortunate in the pastoral care that the boys received from their school. They were never reproached by the school for their tardiness or disorganization. It became a family joke about the amount of phone calls I had to make to the school head of year with the varying and seemingly bizarre explanations for the boy's lateness or absences.

When the boys were at school, I would slowly attend to domestic tasks. I tired easily and it took a long time for me to complete even the most basic of jobs. I was initially worried about leaving the safety of my home. I was worried about any odours that may arise as the colostomy bag filled, or even worse if it would burst. My bag did burst once when I was receiving a remedial massage, and while the massage therapist held me in great dignity, it further compounded my fear of the outside world. I felt like pulling away from everyone and everything in life completely, but I urged myself daily to venture outside my home. I did not want fear to trap me in a closeted world of one building, even if it was my home. Grocery shopping or the occasional lunch with people I felt comfortable with was all I could initially manage. At least these small trips got me out of the house.

I slept during the day after one of my exerting trips out or just to get way from myself and the internal heaviness that was growing as the weeks went on. These sleeps never left me rested when the alarm went off to wake me before the boys came home from school. They seemed to add to the darkness that first visited me in hospital.

One day a colleague from the therapy center I had established came to visit me. She told me at great length about the stress that people in my workplace were going through as a result of my not being there. I was chastised for not listening to their needs or being supportive of what they were going through as a result of my absence. The disappointment felt by some people in how I withdrew into myself during my recovery made me feel that I had let down not just my immediate colleagues but also my clients and other professionals I worked with. The weight of this belief led me to see myself as one colossal failure. Those shards of my former self told me I was responsible for fixing this.

My professional training came to me in waves of accusations: "A healer knows how to hold her own suffering and reach out to others in pain, a social worker is always empathetic and supportive, a narrative therapist can question this dominant story of cancer, the solution-focused practitioner would know how to tap into her own resources."

All the old dictates of my training in professional boundaries came back. I felt it was my duty to ensure that my suffering was kept away from my clients and my professional colleagues. It was my responsibility to protect them all from my pain and not let the two worlds collide.

It was the stuff that mind mazes are made of. I was lost and in pain. Every direction I turned, I could find no way out of this confusion. I tried to challenge these accusations with wisdom from my professional training. I thought about all the literature I had read over the years. I even read an article about self-disclosure after a serious illness.

There was all this professional stuff in my head; it is part of my identity! But the more I grasped at this knowledge, the more it was lost to me. There were no words I read that brought me answers.

I could find no help from my professional knowledge. I heard my colleagues' words of disappointment in me circle constantly in my head. I began to doubt my ability to ever be a therapist again. I had always experienced myself and received feedback from others that I was a skilled and caring person. Now it seemed some questioned my worthiness to do the work. I felt in every part of my being that the remnants of my known identity were shattered beyond recognition.

The voices of collegial criticism and the lack of professional wisdom dragged me deeper and deeper into a maze, only to find an oppressive aloneness that characterized my life. As a result, I did not return to work for seven months instead of the two to three months I had estimated for recovery from the surgery. All the time I was struggling with my professional failings, I was also struggling with my personal failure.

Beyond the world of rational thought lies the realm of raw human emotion, which all of us reside in from time to time. The journey there is not chosen deliberately, it happens in the flicker of automatic moments of living. It seemed that the disappointment my colleagues felt in me had opened the floodgates to self-reproach. I was flung into the rawness of feeling I had hurt and let down the people I loved, which was far greater than the physical pain from the operation.

My mind played over and over the phone call the night I told my mother and father that I had to be operated on for colon cancer. My father answered the phone, and as I told him the news, he silently listened. But when my mother came to the phone, she asked me what I had told him, as she could not get any words out of him because he was crying. I have only seen my father cry twice in my life, so I knew when she told me this his distress must have been great. I saw Roisin, whom I had asked to look after the boys, sitting on my back veranda and crying after I told her. And I could see the shock, the discomfort, and the sadness in many of the faces of people I had told.

Moreover, I carried the image of the fear on my youngest son's face when he first visited me in hospital just after the morphine incident. The script of parenting my two children I had been following did not prepare me for this. It did not prepare me for being the cause of pain and distress to my two children. I was always strong and knowing, protective, and caring. I had supported them through the difficulties of the last two years. They could turn to me for anything, and I would always be there and support them. I had now abandoned them to cancer, and they were alone.

Many months later when we were sheltered in the safe harbor of full recovery my sons and I spoke of this time. The eldest one told me of the aloneness he experienced through that time. He spoke with a depth that was beyond his twelve years. My youngest child spoke about his fear of my dying and how he could not imagine life without me. I listened to their words and talked with them as meaning emerged and their life was strengthening by their experience.

But during this time I could not quiet the internal accusations or stop the physical pain in my chest that reminded me I was the cause. Nothing eased this torment, and I felt as if I would drown in the guilt of causing this pain to those I loved. I felt unworthy of the love and help that was showered on me by friends, as I could not return it. They cooked for me, cleaned, and lovingly cared for my children. I was no longer the heart and soul of a party, always planning some social event, or provider of a loving helping hand to my friends. I could barely find laughter or find the energy to do mundane domestic chores. I was not who I knew I was in connection to them. I was struggling. I knew they were acting from love. I could not have managed without them, so I surrendered to their care. But at the same time, I found no avenue to acknowledge that I felt I had betrayed my part of the friendship bargain that had a self-imposed clause that said, "Do not burden."

I started noticing that I was becoming more unfamiliar to myself in other spheres of my life.

I love earthly beauty: the form of plants, the contours of towering mountains, and the grace of speeding animals. Their beauty moves me to great joy. But now all I saw were objects. Each one was no different from the other, and they were void of all their unique beauty. They left me unmoved.

I love nothing better than a good time: laughing with people I love, watching a movie, and dancing with uncoordinated freedom. But this all seemed meaningless. There was no joy in these pursuits anymore.

I wondered if this Mary Jo who lived in a silent darkness and did not enjoy the things of her previous existence came into being the day I had betrayed her in the hospital ward by not knowing how to write her name. Or was it that my work colleagues questioned my value as the founder of the therapy practice? I told no one of these feelings at the time. It seemed too bizarre to put language to it, so I performed in the body of the Mary Jo that everyone related to.

This place of feeling a failure to myself and others was at times oppressive. And at other times, it would lift for a moment, an hour, or a day. Some mornings, I would wake up from my sleep and be amnesic to what I was experiencing, but as sleep retreated, I would remember and the internal silent darkness would return. There did not seem to be a pattern to how oppressive the experience would be from moment to moment or day to day.

In desperation, I felt if I had a name for my experience, perhaps then an identity would come back, just as the identity of "patient" when I was on the ward helped at times to keep the darkness from swallowing me. I actively sought the wisdom of others, as I could not trust this self I was unfamiliar with to know what was wrong with me.

One doctor diagnosed me with acute reactive depression, the other with clinical depression type "something or other," and they prescribed me Zoloft and "something or other." Perhaps this wasn't too bad a label. I had, after all, a name for this darkness that rolled in and out of my days, and it meant I wasn't going mad or just being downright self-indulgent! In the flotsam and jetsam of this search for meaning, my emotions were also being tossed around by guilt. When the darkness was not so oppressive, I felt guilty that I was expressing any negative sentiments. I realized that many more people suffered far greater agonies than me. I was surviving cancer—two operations saw to it that I was in recovery—and there was no chemotherapy or radiotherapy to endure, so I had no right not to be celebrating my good fortune.

I sat alone by the river, in my bed, on a heap on the kitchen floor or at the base of the washing line after my children went to school. I cried with no one there and no wisdom to guide me. Nothing to cling to in ease of this despair. A vast aloneness spread out in all directions within me and beyond me. My soul was lost to the darkness, and it felt like I would never discover the way out.

Identity that I thought was fixed, the one I had come to know as me, was taking a hammering. Looking back at that time, I have come to realize that it was not just the diagnosis and the medical intervention I went through that caused the enfolding darkness to go so deep. It was the fact that I felt I had failed everyone. This was fuelled especially by the words and deeds of some my work colleagues. They undermined my role as the founding principal and voiced their displeasure to me and others at my lack of support for them.

In terms of my identity, this was my darkest hour. The feedback from my work colleagues surely was the evidence of my inadequacy as a social worker and the head of a team. I questioned my social-work identity and my worthiness. I was being a mechanical mother and not a heart-felt, fully engaged "mama" that I wanted to be. My boys seemed to be going through their daily life without problems, but I questioned if I had somehow damaged their sense of security or affected their well-being, and I did not have the will to discuss it with them. I was failing them. My connection to friends seemed to be all about my needs, and I was giving nothing back in return. I questioned why they would even stay in my life.

This spiralling darkness in this phase of my life sucked away any light that could possibly illuminate my value as a person. The evidence of my unworthiness was daily, and there seemed to be no guidance available to help me through.

Chapter 11

The Way through
the Darkness

My journey through the darkness of despair to the light of engaging more fully in life did not occur as a brilliantly illuminated moment or flash of deep insight. It happened within the movement of days coming and days going. I did not apply any techniques specifically to "recover." I merely lived life's unfolding ways. The way out also did not happen in any linear fashion. I lived in a backward/forward continuum ranging from some minutes, hours, or days of recovery to total darkness. Now looking back, I see that some of the things that helped me came gently and slipped in and out of my days unnoticed by me at the time. Others slowly and progressively unfurled in front of me, and others tapped me on the shoulder and told me what to do. Or they came from deep inside with deliberate intent to act.

Through my recovery, I made a discovery about emotional darkness. I found out what happens at the edges of darkness. I found out what to do where it ends. At the edge where light and dark touch each other and are neither one nor the other, I could stand and notice a different landscape from the one I had been immersed in. I could see the light beyond the darkness and imagine myself standing in it. In the light, I found some of my previous knowledge and courage and heaps of support for myself and from others, but most of all I discovered love.

From within the broken pieces of my identity, I slowly started to notice little bits of my former personality traits. I found within me a determination to go beyond mere survival and find a way back to me. I was always one for creative solutions, and one such was my fake-it-until-you-make-it ploy. I decided to experiment with it to see if anything would flow.

All who know me are familiar with my love of walking. I use it to meditate, exercise, wind down after a day's work, for sheer enjoyment, or for any excuse I can come up with. When I felt emotionally and physically strong enough to leave the safety of my home, I began my walks again. My walks took me around the water's edge of the Parramatta River in my "Zoloft shuffle." I so named it because of the lumbering pace at which I walked, the lack of joy which I noticed was upon me during these walks, and the relationship I formed with the medication I was given at the time of my diagnosis of depression. I had decided that before I took any tablets that I would experiment with trying to release the "feel good chemicals" I needed for recovery. I was not dismissive of taking the medication. My duty to recover for my children and others who depended on me made sure that if pills were to be popped, pills would be popped. But first I wanted to give it a go my way.

During my walks, I stopped to look at native birds and bush or the sun glinting on water. Nature and the bounties of this beautiful earth are among my great loves. In those early days after leaving hospital, as I looked at all that was on offer, I felt nothing—not the slightest echo of my former love or thump of that ancient Irish heartbeat of my spirit.

Some days, I would stare coldly at vivid bottlebrush or busy parakeets with a distant gaze disconcerting in its detachment. Other days, my lack of connection to my former love would cause me to sit at the river's edge and cry in huge gulping sobs, caring not for who saw me; my grief was inconsolable. Indelibly imprinted on my soul now is the knowledge learnt during that time. Beauty is not seen with the eyes. It is felt with the heart. But then there was a great gaping hole that had once been filled with the feeling of seeing beauty.

Even though no feeling came, I would stop to look. I would take time to be near bush and bird. I did not know how to fill this gaping hole. All I knew was that filling it was not a process that could be forced or manufactured, but I chose to "fake it until I make it." I knew that for now, I could stand and look and see beauty, even if I could not feel it and could not stop the flow of tears at my loss. My engaging in my "for now" practice accepted that for now the knowledge, not the feeling of beauty, would have to suffice and that hopefully one day the pain of the loss would go away. For now, I could look.

Eventually, exalting joy and my deep spiritual connection to the earth and all her natural gifts did return. I can't name a day or a moment. It returned in a shy and faltering way but eventually took up more permanency within me as time passed. I do remember the day that I noticed, as I was looking at a bottle bush that the day before, and the day before that, I had felt beauty and these quiet stirrings had gone unnoticed in me until that minute. And again I sat by the river's edge and cried, as I am crying now writing this. The incredible joy, the sense of grateful humility that I felt and still feel now, that the beauty of nature had once again been revealed to me spilled over in my tears and filled me. This love had returned.

On those mornings when I would not recognize the self I woke up to, or failed to connect to what I once loved, I made an effort to participate in activities, look at old photos, or rummage through memorabilia that reminded me of happier times. At first, it was a mechanical process. But internal whispers told me of the importance of keeping this connection alive. The internal whispers were indeed wise. Eventually, from small flickers of connection in the dark, the light went on. I began to feel the experiences I had lived in the photographs again. I began to regain the self that was contained within them.

Many people gave me words of love and encouragement, telling me to get better for myself or take time for myself. Despite being deeply grateful for their encouragement, their words rang meaningless in my ears. I needed to get through this darkness first and foremost for my children, Cadhla and Conor. I also wanted to relieve my family fear of this genetic story of cancer. I wanted my friends to feel no worry, *and* I wanted to get back to myself, but *self* came way after others. I discovered through cancer how deep my love for others is and how strong my belief in service to other is in my work. I chose my way, and it was a way of love for others.

The more I embraced my love for others, the more I was able to receive their gifts of love back to me. One (or should I say two) of the greatest gifts of relationship and love came from Cadhla and Conor. It wasn't just that I noticed they were being a bit more helpful and attentive to me. It wasn't just that they were the biggest part of my reason to get through the darkness. It was also the ordinary ways of our love for each other. I knew that the three of us were fundamentally changed by this experience but we also remained unchanged. They still harassed me about having more computer time, squabbled with each other as siblings do, and left wet bath towels on the floor that had me practicing my banshee mother skills. It was this still being themselves that was the greatest gift of love.

We also discovered that the travelling buddies that we had become during our Australian holidays was to enter a whole new chapter. Before I returned to work, I had a decision to make: to reinvest the last little bit of savings I had left or go on a holiday somewhere special with the boys. I knew how much I had enjoyed travelling through Laos and Cambodia. When I was there, I knew how much I wanted to share these experiences with the boys. Therefore, it was not a decision that took long to take.

So in January 2008, we went to Laos and Vietnam. We had more fun than I imagined, and our relationship was cemented even more tightly. Despite some of the little pressures of travelling, there were few arguments and we seemed to fall into a synchronicity that made the holiday sublimely happy. Cadhla described us as perfect travelling companions, "Because I am good at directions, Conor is good at bartering, and Mama, you have the credit card."

The love from others also came when oppressive loneliness visited and revisited me. I sought the company of people I loved.

Their mere physical presence helped, particularly when they did not expect me to give too much of myself. My stunning friends seemed to instinctively know that I just needed to be near them without contributing to the relationship at that point. The guilt I felt at feeling a failure as a friend, because it was not reciprocated, melted away under the incredible warmth and acceptance of their love. I learnt to accept help from friends with grace and not feel a failure to them. I surrendered to the love that they wanted to give in all its forms.

I can still hear the chatter and laughter of all the women who unpacked my house for me. I remember Liz coming into my home one day and instructing me to sit while she made me a cup of tea and did my ironing, and then she was gone without hardly drawing breath. Another friend Bronwyn came over to my home one night just to make me a cup of tea because I had told her the night before I was so tired I could not lift my head off the sofa to make myself my favourite nightcap of chamomile tea. I can see other girlfriends bringing me dinner despite the busy schedule they had with their own families. They did all this, and much more, without the slightest hesitation and as if it was the most natural thing in the world to do, next to breathing.

There was the unwavering companionship of my adoring dog, Toby. The week before I was diagnosed I chastised him for the constantly pushing his nose into my stomach, hanging around my heels to the point that I tripped up and looking up at me too much with a seemingly worried look on his face. But in my days of healing I never pulled away from his nosey nudges, his curling at my feet or laying his head in my lap as I cried. His silent care held me together more often than not.

The relationship with my surgeon Matthew was a very significant part of my healing. I appreciated not just his skill with a surgical blade but his compassion and human kindness. It took away the barrier that stood between patient and doctor without violating the ethics of that relationship.

He did so in the simple ways of how he spoke to me and the manner in which he approached me. But more importantly, he was also able to embrace my resistance to the totality of the patient label, whether he realized he was doing this or not. I purposefully refused the totality of the label as if a stubborn streak in me tiptoed in under the radar of my conscious thought!

One of the most significant of these moments was when I asked him if I could get access to the operating theatre where I had had the cancer removed. I needed to walk into that room of my own volition, not be wheeled in on a trolley while anesthetized with chemicals. I told him that I needed to reclaim that part of me, that part of my spirit that was left behind. I knew within every fibre of my being that if I did not do this, the darkness that visited me would never fully go away.

He did not press me for further details or call for a psychiatric consult! Instead, for the last of my operations with him, I was wheeled on the trolley to the preparation room, but before they injected the anaesthetic, he came beside me as I got up off the trolley and walked into the operating room beside him, equal in our humanity. I got to see the room and all the equipment that had been used, and would be used again, to save my life. More importantly, I got to say hello to the team who would be involved in the operation.

That long-short walk bridged the gap between physical and spiritual healing I so needed in order to fully come back to knowing myself. It bridged the gap between the doctor-patient hierarchy I so needed to rebalance my feeling of inadequacy. As I walked that short distance beside him into the room I walked a long way back into my internal being. I was home. To all who cling so desperately only to clinical wisdom, take one step towards considering the possibility that there is more to healing. My surgeon did so, and the healing was (and is still within me) immeasurable.

A large part of my time in, and coming out of, the darkness was spent connecting in my heart and mind to my spiritual and ancestral roots. I would move between experiencing total abandonment by my ancestors and spiritual guides to spending hours talking either in silent conversations with them or in their presence loudly keening this pain that had no name.

One such occasion was on the day I had to go to the bank and withdraw a large proportion of the money I had saved. I had no income, minimal child support, and was still carrying the lion share of the expenses to run my therapy centre. I knew this money was needed to keep me and the boys going until I returned to work. With the escalating price of houses, I knew as I withdrew this money I would never be able to buy a home for my sons.

I held the anguish inside while I signed the papers at the bank. When I got home, I shouted out to the stillness in the house. I wanted it to listen to me about yet another thing in life that caused me pain. What returned from my shouts was not an answer but a strong physical sensation of knowing. I felt gratitude. Gratitude that I had this money to fall back on, that I was not living in poverty and homelessness. My shout became my prayer to those whose suffering was far greater than mine was.

I never found glib answers or solutions as a result of these conversations between my audible despair and the quiet. I did not know what to expect back. I did not think divine intercession would intervene to give me money, make the colostomy bag disappear, send my colleagues enlightened thoughts, or recruit my thinking so I would not feel so negative about myself. I just needed spiritual company, and looking back now, I see how often and how present they were with me. It was most particularly in the times when I stopped writhing against my pain and surrendered to its current existence in my life that I felt them around me. It seems like I needed to connect with my spiritual friends and support systems, no different from how I needed to connect to my earthly friends and support systems—just surrender to their presence.

I wonder now if that the lack of hope I experienced in the darkness and the absence of love I experienced in the loneliness left me with nothing but faith. I would not have named it so at the time, but looking back and recalling the day when I spoke to myself and my ancestral spiritual support, and said that I could get through this time if it had meaning, was the day I now know to be the naming of my faith. For in that call for meaning, I see the living hope and purposeful love that I bring to my relationships, my work, and my life. If I were to give it the name *faith*, then it is a faith of love.

While my personal life was being restored through the healing of my identity and the magic of love all around me, my professional life still had to be dealt with. I knew that I could not go back to work at the time that my colleagues expected me to return. I had ongoing professional commitments to people, and I did not want them left in uncertainty. I wanted them to be able to plan the rest of their year without having to wait to hear whether I would be part of this. I wanted to give people an explanation for my delayed return to work with integrity but without burdening them. This brought me back into that mind maze and the accusations: "Keep personal and professional separate." "Don't show your flaws." "Don't be self-indulgent." "Be professional . . . be professional . . . be professional . . ."

I remember standing in the midst of this confusion and screaming, "What does that mean, "Be professional"? From deep within this self-doubt and loss in the darkness, a calmness came over me, and along with it, clarity. I found the courage to write one of the most honest letters I have ever penned. I wrote individually to all my colleagues, teams, and all the other professionals who used my service and explained why I was not returning at the time I originally said I would.

In this letter, I wanted my words to truly portray what was in my heart and on my mind. Although I could not currently find within me the whole person I used to be, I wanted the words in the letter to be as close to who she was as possible. To counteract the lie I felt I was living in relation to my profession, I wanted to give them the truth from my heart. I cried solidly as I hunched over the keyboard. It started with a quote from Kahil Gibran that reminds us that the seed that cannot face the turbulence of the seasons cannot push up through the soil to enjoy the delights of growth in the sun.

The response to that letter took my breath away. I received an outpouring of goodwill from my colleagues. At first, as I read the words they wrote, it sounded like distant whispers telling me that I had worth and value. The connection to them was muted. So I would hold their responses tightly, hoping the sentiments within the ink would seep into my being, and it did. The words to me were much more than expressions of sympathy; they were an unexpected and unsought source of strength and hope.

The letter I wrote, and the responses I received, tapped into a deep well of human compassion and a spirit; it tapped into all that is beautiful in my profession. I received so much more than human sympathy or the empathy we were trained to use. I received the depths of human connection. I was showered with the healing gifts of people who did not judge my journey into the dark as a personality flaw and people who did not harry me to return stoically to work. I found no pressure to do anything, give anything, or produce any measurable contribution to their lives. I did not have to justify the existence of who I was. I found total acceptance of me. My belief in myself as a professional returned through their words of warmth and encouragement.

This time of post-operative recovery brought me into that slipstream of human suffering that flows through us all and connects us beyond the constructed client/therapist or doctor/patient dichotomy. It showed me that my resilience lives in tears, despair, and exploding colostomy bags and in stubbornness, humour, faking, and resisting, as well as in relationships that love me and love me again so that I can make it meaningful in service of others for the love of others.

Chapter 12

The Wisdom of
the Mountain

Several months after my last surgery were the Christmas holidays of 2007, and it was the boys' year to share Christmas with their father. I decided to go to Peru to see my friend who lived in Iquitos and then join a small tour group that would include a walk along the Inca Trail to Machu Picchu. I was forty-nine and not in peak health, so some of my friends lovingly voiced concern at my physical ability to do so. They spoke wise words. While the Inca Trail is not one of the most arduous treks in the world, it could be for a woman of my age who was not in peak physical condition and was recovering from a series of major operations. I listened, but I knew I had to go. I had long wanted to see Machu Picchu. My healing and spiritual journey was continuing, and I knew this was a mountain path I wanted to walk as part of it. The toughest walk I had ever done in my life included the four steps to the end of the hospital bed on the second day my sons visited me. So despite my friends' loving words, I knew I had walked my toughest mountain on behalf of my sons. Now I needed to walk this Peruvian mountain on behalf of myself.

As we flew into Peru, I looked down at stunning cinnamon and clay-coloured mountain ranges with snowed-capped peaks, sloping valleys, and green fields. I was at peace and knew there would be many good times ahead of me in Peru.

After spending a week with my friend, I headed to Lima, where I met the group of people I was to spend the next three weeks with. Our group of six was made up of five tourists and our guide: Peter, a teacher from Sydney; Anthony and Joanne, a graphic designer and a librarian from Melbourne; Rachel, a doctor from New Zealand; and Marco, our local guide. After our tour briefing in the hotel we stayed at, we went out for our first of many meals together. I was at ease with these strangers and continued to be comfortable with them throughout our time together.

After spending a few days in Lima together, we headed off, staying at Nasca and Arequipa before getting to Cusco.

Nasca was dry, and the dust clung to me with grim hope; it tasted unpleasantly musty in my mouth. But the thrill of stepping into a six-seater airplane muted my discomfort. Out travelling group had boarded this plane to view the famous Nasca lines, which were vast outlines of shapes etched into the landscape by the ancient inhabitants of this land. I had longed to see these shapes ever since I had heard of them many years ago, and I was not disappointed by the beauty of their vastness or awe at their creation so long ago. I did mention the motion sickness caused by the swoops and turns of the plane, didn't I?

Fascinated as I was by this age-old land art, Nasca will stay memorable for me because of our afternoon trip. We drove to a pre-Inca archaeological site in the middle of a flat, windswept, arid landscape. The distant mountains rising upfrom the shimmer of heat bouncing off the earth. I felt strangely drawn to these mountains and started walking in their direction, only to be called back by our guide. He wanted me to walk with the rest of the group towards a series of wood-covered walkways.

I took no more than two steps forward when I was pushed by an overwhelming sense of sadness and the sound of distance lamenting in my ears. My heart ached so much that it took my breath away. I started to cry as if I was grieving the death of someone dear to me. I didn't see any reason for what was happening to me and could not explain myself when Marco came over to me. Looking at me, he said, "They are attracted to you like the moths to the light." I was puzzled as to who was attracted to me and for what purpose. He explained that the site was a burial ground. Several of the tombs had been excavated, the skeletons exposed for tourists to visit. Marco said their spirits were calling to me.

I had a similar experience the year before when I visited Laos. I was walking around the parameters of a temple when the same overwhelming feeling of grief struck me and tears of sorrow started to flow. My guide told me that the rock I was standing beside, just as this happened, was where they threw the bodies of the young women they had just sacrificed.

Since then, these two incidents have not been the only ones of their type. I wonder if the energy of someone suffering stays present long after he or she is gone and that my experience in the hospital bed, where I connected to all of human suffering, makes me more open to picking this up emotionally, regardless of the passing of time.

From Nasca we travelled to Arequipa. I fell in love with Arequipa- her narrow streets, sun-filled squares, cathedral steps, arched doorways, ringing church bells, and her easy feel. I loved her so much that I spent two days on my own while the rest of the group took a short trip outside the city. I spent my days in happy wanderings through the streets, discovering tucked-away cafes, peaceful churches, and rooftop vistas from which to sit and sip my wine in the lone company of a blazing, setting sun.

Cusco was our next port-of-call. In Cuzco, visits to Inca temples, Catholic churches, and hilltop vistas are a great source of fun and interest to me. Walking through the main town square that night, lit by the restaurants and shops and the sloping cape of lights from the surrounding hills, filled me to bursting with joy. I wanted to shout at the top of my voice, "I'm in Cuzco, Peru! I'm alive to enjoy all of this!" But I restrained myself with, instead, a permanent grin on my face and zealous banter with my travelling buddies.

From Cusco, we started our trekking tour to Machu Picchu. Each walking group had porters who carried the tents, camping equipment, and food supplies throughout the trek. We carried the duffle bags provided, which weighed the compulsory six kilograms or below. So I headed off on the four-day trek with one pair of shorts, one pair of trousers, two pairs of socks, four pairs of knickers, four T-shirts, a toothbrush, tooth paste, and a face cloth. Travelling through south-east Asia on my way to Australia some twenty years previously, I thought I had learnt to travel light, but this was the most minimalist I have ever been.

We were fortunate to walk the trail with a guide who showed us the natural bounties of the mountain, her orchids hidden behind large clumps of overgrowth, humming birds busy at work at the entrance of a blossom, and sacred stone carvings left behind by the Inca worshippers. He shared with us the precious gift of his cultural and spiritual wisdom, of Pachamama, the mountain goddess. I loved the fact that I was miles away from Ireland and he spoke of the Inca connection to goddesses and gods of mountains and rivers and sea and sky, just as we Celts had done hundreds of years ago.

The first day of the trek was Christmas day. As I opened my eyes, I opened my heart, and pain of not being with my two sons came pouring out. I had been unable to speak to them the day before to give them my Christmas love, leaving only a message on a distant-sounding answering machine. I missed them, and I sensed they missed me. Months later, my eldest son was to tell me that my youngest cried bitterly when he heard my phone message. Perhaps this sadness I felt was not mine alone.

The day started as a day of tidal proportions, washing waves of differing emotions back and forth through my heart. There were times on that day when I gave in to the tears and simply allowed my footsteps to follow the heavy, falling drops of my tears. There were other times when the weight of missing them was so great that I thought I could not move forward. Then there were other times where peace would settle for a while and my walking was unhindered.

I neither gave into the burden of each emotion nor ignored it. I neither celebrated the peaceful moments nor harried them guilty away. I simply walked in time to my own emotional and physical rhythm and let everything be as it was. As the day unfolded, I noticed dual existence within me: hope sat alongside my despair, joy alongside my sadness, and love alongside the emptiness. Missing my children and knowing I would be with them again could sit side by side, and this accompanied me along the mountain that day.

When we set out on each leg of the walk, we always set out together, and it quickly became clear that some of us walked at a faster pace than others did! Initially, I thought my job was to keep up with the others and stay in the group. But I found it impossible; youth and physical fitness were not with me in body. I found I dropped back quite quickly.

I did not reproach myself. Instead, I settled into this beautiful rhythm with my own heartbeat and breathing, and I found an incredible meditative pace as foot moved before foot.

The joyful peace of that walking pace was potent. This peace erased the need to move any faster or any slower. I saw I had no cause to be any walker on that mountain track other than who I was. It was a blissful happiness to finally acknowledge that I needed to be no one but myself and the most important of all the things in life was to be myself.

I was on my own at times, with people at other times moving in and out of shared and solo pacing, but I was never alone. I moved in deep connection at times with my walking group, my family and friends back at home, my family and spiritual ancestry, my beloved nature, and myself.

I enjoyed being part of my Inca walking companions. Rachel, young and fit, would take off on each leg of the trail at a rapid pace and arrive first at each meeting point. One day, she asked me how it was possible that I walked so slowly yet always reached our destination points only minutes after her and the other fast walkers. My smile in reply was as large as the look of puzzlement on her face when I told her I walked to my own pace and not the pace of anyone else. I spoke of following the steady beat of my own heart, not that of any other beating heart. I told her that I not only followed my own internal music but I enjoyed its unique melody.

By the second day of the trek, the emotional pain had eased somewhat, but the physical task had increased in difficulty. Initially, I looked far ahead of me to the pinnacle, where I was to meet the others, and was almost overwhelmed by the distance and the thought that I would not make it. As I began to walk, I noticed quite quickly that when I looked too far ahead, I immediately felt the tyranny of distance and the seemingly impossible task for me to cover it. I could see that others appeared to effortlessly meet this challenge, and I began to negatively compare myself. My pace slowed, my energy drained from my body, and my breathlessness increased. I also noticed when I dropped my head and took my gaze from the pinnacle to my feet that I tripped or stumbled on an obstacle in front of me on the path that I had no advance warning of. I was too unsure of my foothold. I moved forward too slowly, my muscles depleted of their strength. The newfound wisdom of the day before that told me to listen to myself directed me to set my sights to just the level of my line of vision.

I came to realize that looking too far ahead was me looking at someone else's achievement and not my own, at a task too big and sapping of my energy. Looking close to my feet gave me no sense of purposeful walking or where to move to, and hence I faltered.

When I lifted my head to an angle that blocked out the tyranny of visual distance and gave me a clear line of vision forward, I neither stumbled nor drained of energy. I did not get tired or want to give up. I did not walk slowly or push myself out of my pace. In unison with my own pace, I achieved balance and a walking energy that allowed me to focus on an achievable piece of ground to cover.

As I started to allow the joy of this discovery to fuel me, I noticed the most wonderful of things. I noticed that just at the level that my eyes focused was the mountains' beauty—flowers, butterflies, humming birds, rock formations, and at one time a gently flowing river. Looking too far into the distance or too close to the feet, the eye could not see this beauty. I giggled silently (and perhaps not so silently at times), about this discovery, and I wondered if the mountain knew to do this. Did the mountain know that along the journey, encouragement and not despair was needed? I wondered at the magnificence of the placing of this beauty just at the right level for my eye, just the right amount of beauty to inspire the next footstep to see what I would discover. And so I settled into walking the Inca Trail in the rhythm of my own body, energized by knowing that I had only to walk the next lot of steps to see what new beauty lay in waiting for me. The end of the trail would wait for me until I got there.

On the third day of the trail, rain pounded down on us for most of the journey, seeming to increase in intensity with every step. The undulation of the land was not hard to walk on that day, but the rainy conditions made it an arduous walk. I hiked as I had done the days before, following my own rhythm. That was the only day I arrived into camp ahead of the rest of the group. Not because I wanted to or tried to but because the external conditions did not change my internal rhythm and my walking ability was not affected. Rachel found it difficult to walk that day. She said that what finally got her through the day was remembering what I had told her about following her own rhythm. She struggled but she got through.

On the fourth day of the trail, we woke at 4 a.m. to make the final leg of our journey. As light seeped through the darkness and the sun slowly burned away the mist, my anticipation gathered with the knowledge I would within hours be stepping on the ancient ground of Machu Picchu.

I was standing on my own when the mist lifted and I saw Machu Picchu for the first time. I cried. I cried at the immense beauty I saw. I cried in acknowledgment for the lost ancestry of the Inca people. And I cried for myself. I stood in the presence of my ordinary beginnings in the streets of Belfast, the pain of my shattered life after marriage, the presence of a cancer in my body, yet here I am standing on the ancient ground of the Incas. I am alive and get to see all this beauty. I cry. I am deeply grateful.

I allowed these tears of gratitude to flow freely.

Throughout that Inca Trail, throughout all the walks I have ever done on mountains, I have always trusted the land to hold my weight. I have allowed myself to place my foot on her and known she would not trick me with moving form or shifting movements—that is, if I placed my foot wisely and stayed informed about the stability of the land. I am aware that not all parts of this great planet are so solid, or so reliable. There are swamplands, shifting sands, and erupting volcanoes, but I do not chose to walk on them. These are lands that do not will us to walk upon them. The mountain lands I have walked upon are solid lands and have been walked upon for generations before me.

My trust in the mountain, indeed on walking upon any part of this beautiful world, is faith in its form, in being what it is, not its permanency. Mountains like everything wear away with time. That is part of their existence.

I learnt from these mountain walks to honour the form of who I was and who I continue to be. The mountain does not say to me, "Swim upon me, for I wish to be a river." It simply provides the ground beneath my feet by being who it is. For many years of my life, I wanted to be different from who I was—to be more beautiful, more intelligent, more patient, more kind, more . . . But I am not "more." I am me. Walking on the mountain and having this faith in its presence, I opened up faith in myself to be who I am and allow love for that self to keep growing.

Walking alone along the Inca Trail allowed me to look at snapshots of moments and experiences over the last number of years of my life. I noticed that throughout my darkest times, the presence of love was strongest, even when I did not see it or did not call it this.

I am not a woman who is accustomed to reaching out regularly for help. I am by nature self-reliant and strong. But the gift of the difficult times I went through is that they allowed me to ask for and receive help. My friends gave help in different forms, as it was different forms of help I needed. I have heard that at times of need that "it is casseroles that are needed more than counselling." I found that it was both I required depending on my need at the time.

In my difficult times, I not only saw myself held and carried through by family and friends but also a community of working people (nurses, cleaners, doctors, gardeners) that made it possible for me to get through and live a meaningful life. I recall one member of this community of people vividly. Nurses were allocated to help with teaching about care of aperture and perturbing organ, which involves washing it and changing the colostomy bag. On the first day of this instruction, I stood naked in the stark, impersonal hospital shower room beside a nurse.

I still had the catheter to collect my urine and the colostomy bag full of my other waste products; my naked, frail, and imperfect body contrasted against her clothed, strong, and professional body. As she washed my body that I was too weak to wash, as she removed my colostomy bag that I was too unskilled to do, I was intensely sobbing. I was useless as a human being. Through my heavy sob—"That's right, you let it all out, darlin'"—a beautiful, soft-toned Irish voice soothed me.

Her name was Mary, and at the most broken, the most ugly, and the most undignified moments I have ever had in my life, I felt the presence of grace, dignity, and beauty. I looked back from the mountain walk in Peru and saw the two of us in unison, humanity holding humanity, person holding person, and I saw it differently.

I saw not my broken self but the grace, dignity, and beauty of love. I felt that if in doing her job, as she had done many days before, she could hold me and tend to me, then perhaps there was something beautiful in me after all. I was captivated by the thought on that mountain walk that in my most unloving moments of self I could experience myself as most full of grace, dignity, and beauty. I believe that is what she brought to me that day in the shower room. I believe it is what many in my life have brought to me and what continues to fill and sustain me—a beautiful source of love, a love audacious enough to love in the most broken, the most ugly, and the most undignified of times.

Chapter 13

Per Ardua

In 2010, some four years after the episode with cancer began, the boys and I went to Hawaii on yet another one of our holiday adventures together. Before we went, I told some of my friends of the strong sense I had that something was waiting for me. What I did not tell my friends was that I knew love was waiting for me. In my more capricious moments, I thought it was romantic love. I was to discover a greater love than this.

On one of our days out, we explored some lava tunnels. Standing at the end of them when all other tourists had turned back, I begged my son's indulgence to follow my instructions. These boys are accustomed to their mother's eccentricities, so when I asked them to turn off their torches and stay silent, they agreed with that good-natured "Let's humour Mama again" look on their faces. We were alone deep underground, immersed in a velvety darkness and surrounded with silence except for a gentle, steady drip of water that intruded into this peace. The total absence of light meant there was no difference in the quality of the darkness whether your eyes were open or closed. I chose to close my eyes to help me appreciate the stillness of the moment, and as I did so with a gentle immediacy, I felt my body merge with the darkness. My last experience of merging with darkness had happened in a hospital bed some two and a half years before. It was an experience characterized by pain and aloneness connecting me beyond my own anguish to all universal human suffering.

This cave experience was the opposite. It was safe. I smiled. I was instantly at peace. Emerging from within this tranquillity came a presence I knew as love. It was a deep, eternal love that I recognized I had known all my life and had felt in varying intensity throughout the whole of my life. My deep spiritual connection to this source of love made itself first known to me when I was a child. I told no one then, and though I had been in its presence many times as an adult, I hesitantly told only a few.

As love's presence gathered around me, it was as though my body melted away. I became one with the darkness. With the dissolving of this physical barrier of my body, I moved effortlessly into this energy field of love. Being part of this flowing love, I felt fusion with generations of others from every part of the world, every time in history. It was a physical phenomenon as real as the ground beneath my feet and damp cave air entering my nostrils. Even as I write these words, I am privy to its presence.

I knew then that there was no limit to this source of love; no entry to it depended on your race, class, or religious practice. This energy source of love was ever present. It was not profound, overwhelming, or enlightening. It just was peaceful and meant to be.

As I had entered the slipstream of human suffering that night on the hospital bed, I was doing so now into love. I now know how intimately they are both connected, working in unison with each other. These two energy flows of love and suffering seem to belong together, intertwining strands like DNA. They are the double helix of suffering and love that makes us human and that connects us to each other.

The darkness in that Hawaiian tunnel was not an absence of light; it was knowledge. The living knowledge of who I was, am, and will continue to be. Knowledge of the meanings of my life that have been signposted by different experiences. The meanings I came to know from each experience of my lived darkness. In this moment in the belly of the earth, in the presence of this love, I saw into all the darkness of my life from my Belfast childhood to the tumultuous years in my adulthood, and I saw this presence of love waiting patiently for me. It was watching over me.

My family motto is *Per ardua,* which means "through adversity." From first reading the motto on my family crest, I couldn't fully identify with the heraldic message. I am uncomfortable with the ennobling of struggle. I do not subscribe to the notion that my family motto foretells of a divine plan that through adversity I would achieve, survive, or come to know myself. I am not in denial that as a result of the difficult times in my life I have become stronger, more compassionate, and gained more wisdom. However, I am suspicious of trite platitudes that glorify suffering for suffering's sake, shadowing the bitter truth of the depth of human suffering.

Now I have my family crest placed at the entrance to my home. I have found a way to relate to it as I have found a way to relate to the experiences of adversity in my life. In the darkness of times, going through my adversity, I came to see the divine light that is in me and the energy source of love that is all around me.

Alongside my family crest is the plaque that has the name my boys and I choose to have for our home: Le Gra. *Le gra* in Irish means "with love." We gave the house this name so that all who entered it would come with love, and as they left, they would leave with our love. For me it is fitting that each day, as I enter and leave my home, I walk past adversity with love.

This source of love I now honour does not mean that I am protected from the ordinary experiences of life. Indeed, the daily mechanics of life goes on much as before. Four years after my marriage ended, I found myself in a relationship where I decided to open my heart again to love. I chose to love another man. Almost one and a half years into the relationship, he decided to end it. The haunting spectre of a broken heart revisited me once again. Some of my friends were vigilant in their attendance to my expected distress. But it did not manifest that way. Alongside the pain and loss were a deep peace and what I can almost describe as joy.

My different self, changed by my difficult times and the knowledge that came in the aftermath, saw that in the past it was easy for me to believe in love when love was letting itself be known in a relationship. Now, even with the loss of that relationship, I still feel the presence of love. It does not go away. It is my choice to allow it to flow through me and manifest in many different ways: motherhood, daughter, sister, friendship, work, and romance. I know that just because a certain practice of love is not returned to me or is not engaged in by me, it does not mean that love has gone from my life. I know love is not defined by what society or common wisdom tells us it should look like. I believe that love can be celebrated and practised in many small and grand ways in each of our lives, and how each of us does so is as wonderfully different as we are.

I don't hurt any less than any other person. I don't fall in love more than any other person. I don't have any special, mystic powers that allow me to tap into this source of divine love. What I have done is finally laid claim to that loving energy source I knew existed ever since I was a child. Being in the presence of that love in the darkness was something I had experienced at other times in my life but did not at that time have the courage or audacity to believe in. I now know it is within me and all around me. And if that is true for me, it is true for us all.

My audacious love of the quirkiness in life thoroughly enjoyed the circumstances of this epiphany; in the dark of the cave, I named my light. I found that my family motto spoke less of a resilient growth through adversity but more importantly of a discovery of audacious love through adversity.

It is now a natural progression for me to acknowledge this eternal, audacious love all around me and see its presence in my life and hence my work. I had never been clinically taught about the presence of love in social work or been tutored in how to utilize it for effective client intervention. Yet it is an incredible energy source for my work.

Looking back over my career, I can now put words to what helped me through the difficult times in my working life. It was this eternal, audacious love. An audacious love that I recognize I have known all my life, although as a child, I had no way of knowing how to talk about it. And as an adult professional, I had no language to describe my experience without facing the fear that I would be ridiculed by my peers. Its roots are now anchored deep inside my being, giving me much strength and sustenance, as do the roots of the trees in the forest of my beloved Cave Hill, where I took my childhood walks.

Waiting for me in that cave in Hawaii was not just this audacious love but also the courage to talk about my relationship with it, courage I previously did not have. I came to realize that I have had over my lifetime many experiences of being in the presence of this love. I have spent many years trying to deny or ignore it or listening to other people's explanation of it when I dared to tentatively approach the subject. I got explanations that were reductionist in nature depending on the belief systems of the person who was dispensing the wisdom: religious, scientific, or psychological. I have pulled back from embracing its presence fully until this point in my life for fear of derision from some in my profession.

I have been told that this disparagement is now happening in some quarters. I no longer fear it nor care about a highly regarded repudiation that does not allow me to honour the spiritual wisdom from my Celtic ancestry.

Celtic mysticism has given me the gift of acknowledgment that the psychological, biological, or religious explanations could not. From deep within my cultural/spiritual heritage, I found in the beauty of mystic believes. I love the belief that without us searching the soul comes to find us, care for us, and love. I know mine *found me and cared for me.*

At the surface level, love motivates me to do those awful, mundane tasks that I am not so keen to do. When I tap into this love, it eases and allows me to enjoy those aspects of my job I least enjoy. I can clean the toilets and vacuum the floors. I can write the reports and keep my filing up to date. I can attend meetings and listen to organizations that seem to oppose my work. I can do all of this with as much love, while giving them my full attention, as I do to listening people who entrust their therapeutic journey to me or turn to me for consultation on their clinic work. All my small and big tasks become equally important, because they are part of my demonstrated love.

I look back at the story of my personal and professional development and see it was permeated with a grasping search for certainty and knowledge that would free me from nagging self-doubt and give me legitimacy.

I grabbed at clinical knowledge so that I could appear the most informed. I learnt that science clings tightly to the rigour of what it holds to be right, true, and real because not to do so means facing the unknown.

I grabbed at religious Knowledge. I learnt that religion clings tightly to the rigour of what it holds to be right, true, and real because not to do so means facing the unknown.

When facing the unknown, we have to face ourselves, make choices, make decisions, and follow paths according to ourselves. I discovered when I face the unknown I am held by love.

I held on tightly to both the scientific and the religious at points in my life, but my soul waited patiently for me and let me find myself within that presence of love that will never leave me. And in meeting my own soul, I now know I do not need clinical wisdom or spiritual practices to bolster me up or give legitimacy to my existence. I can embrace my clinical and spiritual wisdom not because I need them but because I want to learn from them.

This learning does not require I give my Celtic self away. It embraces all wisdoms that both enrich me personally and can be used by me on behalf of others.

It is said Buddha, when asked what he did before enlightenment, said, "Chopping wood and carrying water." And when asked what he did after enlightenment, he said, "Chopping wood and carrying water." While I cannot claim full enlightenment like Buddha, I feel the sameness of his life returning to its routine after enlightenment. I am still Mary Jo; I still relate to all the wonderful people who are in my life. I still work in the same profession. I still perform the daily tasks of life. To the onlookers of my life, I may appear no different. To all intents and purposes, they are right, as the mechanical workings of my professional and personal life may seem no different. And while I feel in many ways the same as I always have, I also feel profoundly changed.

I possess all the same vulnerabilities and failings, but I bring a much deeper and more compassionate love to the essence of who I am, particularly those parts I previously found unlovable, those imperfections I judged unworthy of love. If this love, whose presence I felt all my life, deems me worthy, then I must be audacious enough to do so as well.

It is not possible to learn how to ride a bicycle without sitting on the seat and moving forward. In this moving forward, the learner will fall off and may be hurt. The falling off teaches as much about balance and speed and co-ordination as does the staying on; we can't have one without the other. Our failings and our vulnerabilities are the learner part of who we are; without them, there is no *us*. Being perfectly imperfect is part of the continuous flow of life. Finding this audacious love has shown me to approach that part of me that falls off, with great compassion and nurturing.

My family motto of *Per ardua* can be a shared wisdom for everyone, a call to look at personal and professional journeys of adversity and see what lies within and what wisdom can be brought into being as a source of sustenance throughout life. And most important of all, how through adversities love shows us that our worth can be found.

Chapter 14
Living with Audacious Love

*L*ife continues as before: the same routine of being a mother, a work colleague, a sister, and a friend. From the outside, it may not seem as if my life has changed much, and it hasn't. However, from the inside looking out at my world, I am changed and changing. I hold within me many precious gifts from the times of adversity.

The ancient name for Ireland is Eriu, which means "goddess." The ancient Celts saw Ireland as the personification of this goddess and believed that her divine wisdom lies within the land, the mountains, rivers, lakes, and seas. The ancient ways of my far-flung ancestors may have receded in time, but Eriu continues her goddess-like care and wisdom in its land.

When the storms stop raging off the west coast of Ireland and you walk upon early-morning beaches off Dingle Bay, you can sometimes discover—alongside the debris—a wealth of crystals that the storm has washed ashore. This crystal-bedecked scene can only happen after the storm. This storm is ignorant of the garlanded landscape it will produce upon easing. It rages not to decorate; it exists but to be a storm.

I do not adhere to the belief in an interventionist or vengeful deity who sends us trials to test us. I do not believe that we purposefully manifest great difficulties or life-threatening illness to teach ourselves a lesson or for any other "noble" purpose. I believe difficult times are like the storm: difficult in nature and raging at the time of its existence, ignorant of the results that it will produce. However, I do believe that if we are prepared to walk upon the storm-ravaged landscape after the squalls have resided, we may find the jewels washed up on the shore. The jewels that show the hidden treasures of this life. This book is written because of that walk along the shoreline, and to write it, I needed to be prepared to walk upon my internal landscape with eyes wide open to what is there.

I see within myself the jewels revealed after the storm of events abated in my life. These jewels sparkle as joy, hope, beauty and gratitude, and what holds them all together is love. I am not fully in their presence every moment of every day. I still face difficulties in my work and personal life, but I find that I can access these gifts more readily and life has a far happier quality than it ever previously did.

I have learnt through adversity that identity is not fixed; it is a flowing, changing part of who we are. The wisdom of Eriu has taught me that the great rock eventually wears to the grain of sand we enjoy crunching beneath our feet, the gentle sapling grows to be the sturdy tree, and the one drop of rain becomes part of the flowing river. All of life is impermanent, a constantly changing form. But this does not need to be seen as scary. It can also be the agent for growth, change, and expansion.

This may seem hard for people to put into practice, as the thought of an ever changing existence can be daunting for people, particularly as we tend to seek certainty. The belief in the catalytic potential of impermanence need not breed anxiety. It lends itself to an approach that believes in hope. It is a recognition that all of life is changing and hence you too can change. It is recognition that when things are not so fixed, then boundless possibilities exist. It allows for creativity and growth so, rather than white-knuckling through some difficult situations or clinging to what is, you can allow the mind to harness possibilities because things are not permanent, not stuck, and not inevitable. The jewel of hope that I now see not only comes from this new relationship I have with the impermanence of life but also from engaging in acts that allow hope to grow to reality.

As a result of the operations to remove the cancerous growth in my body, I live with a stomach patched with scars, a minor bowel dysfunction, and intermittent pain. I felt my body had betrayed me and I lost faith in it, adding to my loss of faith in myself. I recoiled at the thought of anyone seeing me naked and from doing any exercise in public. Three people were particularly instrumental in helping me regain my faith in my body and thus also helping me with my sense of self.

When I first went to yoga classes at the Concord Studio in Sydney, I was quite frankly terrified of what my body could or could not do in terms of physical dexterity and would or would not do in terms of its bowel dysfunction. Kylie Hennessy, Lynn Moyce, and Mandy Scotney dispelled all these fears and worries. They never forced me into yoga positions or required that I grow, strengthen, or change. They worked with the true philosophy of yoga practice being just that: *a practice,* particularly a personal form of practice. They did not falter in their tuition and guidance even when my tears of disappointment began to flow. They showed me that despite my dismay in my physical status and dysfunction, I could still be taught, and more importantly, I could still learn.

I no longer gingerly step into the yoga studio. I bound joyfully in, ready to get going. My physical dexterity still is not perfect, and my bowel dysfunction has not gone, but the acceptance I got and the encouragement to love my body again sit triumphantly along with it.

While writing this book, I had a minor procedure as preventive measure, which is an ongoing part of my life. Before the procedure, a ritual of fasting and cleansing is required. The morning I woke up to go to the hospital, twinges of hunger rippled through my stomach and awoke in me a poignant realisation. Through my pangs of hunger, I felt connected across time and planet to people I had never and would never meet. My hunger pain was not my pain. It was not a pain of ownership but a connection. It was not a pain of comparison but of recognition. I felt as close to all those who had died of hunger in that moment as if I were nursing them in death. It was not overwhelming.

It felt like pure love. My tears flowed slowly and gently down my face with love for them not sadness for myself. I also felt deep gratitude for all life had brought my way. The joyful and the painful. The jewels from the storms of the last few years. Jewels of experience that connects me to all who walk this earth.

I see everything that happened in my life during those years connects me to each of you reading this. This is not a connection that claims some magical power to know each of you or your experience. It is a connection that knows we all face the storms. A connection that would like my story to help you find your own crystals on your inner shoreline, and you to hold onto the possibilities of what can be, so you can embrace your own audacious love.

I look back and see that I added to these difficult times by giving myself an even harder time! The anger that was heaped on me and the external judgements of others cannot compare to those times of internal criticism that I levelled at myself. I also see that a lot of my suffering came from railing against what I was going through. I see now that there can be no forcing my way through these processes of life, but there is a need to surrender to the moments. This level of surrender to the course of life does not equate to a defeatist attitude that invited me into victimhood. Indeed, it is the opposite. It is an attitude that is full of the deep understanding that some things are to be endured not because I want to endure them but because that is how it is to be.

I have learnt it is important to be the night watchwoman to myself, the one who keeps awake to ensure that the thieves of anguish do not steal my reserves. I have learnt to give myself some relief from any forensic carving away at my life as to where I "went wrong," what I could have done better, or how I could not have seen this coming. This did not serve me well during this difficult time and depleted me of important emotional, physical, and spiritual energy I needed to see me through.

I have learnt the importance of being compassionate and loving to myself when I fall short of my or any others' expectations of how I should act or how I should feel. There are no *shoulds*. Should a baby walk just because it has legs, an emu fly because it has wings, a lake flow instead of being still because it has water? The answers lie within the nature of all these things. They are being as they were intended to be, not walking, not flying, and not flowing. They cannot be other than that, for to be other than that is to be something different. They would be no longer the baby, the emu, or the lake.

As difficult as things get, I learnt an important part of facing difficult times is to be deeply compassionate and loving to all those aspects of my being. This position has the beauty of mercifulness, which speaks lovingly to self. It says to these entire moments of life, "This is where I am and where I am meant to be." And then it lets it be. In this letting be, that presence of audacious love that has sustained me all my life can find me and help me through.

And so looking at where I am now is looking at where I am meant to be. I do not know what tomorrow or the next day brings. I am not a fully enlightened being and have not reached divine perfection. I am like each person who reads this book: fully human. But what I do know is that there is a great source of love flowing around me, with me, and through me. All I have to do each day is choose to step into the centre of this source and act from this place with as much audacity as I can, each and every day. And I know you can do that too.

Written with much *audacious love* to you.

Le gra, Mary Jo

Great Source of Audacious Love

Great source of audacious love
that surrounds me, that knows me, that holds me,

Make me messenger of your presence.
Where there is hatred, let me sow your love.
Where there is injury, pardon.
Where there is doubt, faith.
Where there is despair, hope.
Where there is darkness, light.
Where there is sadness, joy.

O divine energy source,
Remind me of how loved I am.
Send me guidance when I am lost.
Send me remembering when I have forgotten.

Teach me to love as you love.
Teach me to understand as you understand.
Teach me to console as you console me.

For it is in giving that I know I will receive,
In loving that I will be loved,
In spreading joy that joy will be with me.

And so may this always be,
For in this great and wonderful connection
between all living beings your presence will ever be.

(Adapted by Mary Jo with great gratitude for,
and great love of, St Francis of Assisi.)

CPSIA information can be obtained at www.ICGtesting.com
Printed in the USA
LVOW060532210513

334746LV00001B/3/P